HELEN WOOD

A Man's World

ISBN 978-1-906670-51-1

Printed and bound by
CPI Group (UK) Ltd, Croydon, CR0 4YY

Dedicated to my son, and also my best friend Michelle

Bang, bang, bang, bang. Someone was knocking at the door. The next moment, they were hammering at it again.

"Christ, I'm coming!" I yelled, wondering why I couldn't just get one moment of peace. It had been a stressful few weeks and I hadn't slept in ages, but I slid off the sofa anyway – at least if I dealt with this caller, I might get some quiet.

Little did I know, the minute I opened it, things were about to get much worse. My life had been an absolute roller coaster up until this point, and now things were going to get even crazier.

On my doorstep was a man in his thirties, dressed in a suit. I instantly clocked the Dictaphone in his hand.

"Hi, I'm a reporter with the News of the World. I'd like to talk to you about Wayne Rooney." My mouth fell open, and I stared at him as he continued. "We know he paid you to sleep with him last year, and now we'd like to hear your side of it."

Shit. How could this man possibly know?

It was a year since Manchester United's golden boy Wayne had paid me and another girl, Jenny Thompson, to have sex with him. He'd booked us to come to the Lowry hotel in Salford for a threesome. It hadn't been the most memorable sex, but because he was an England star, it had obviously stood out. But I'd not told a single person other than my best friend Michelle, and I wanted it to stay that way, so who the hell was this guy to suddenly ask me about it now?

"What the fuck are you on about? Don't knock on this door again!" I barked, before slamming the door and stumbling back inside, thoughts racing through my head.

Collapsing onto my sofa, I tried to take deep breaths to calm myself and stop from being sick. I thought about the life I'd fought so hard to build with my son. Some people might think it was mediocre, but to me, we'd gone from living on the breadline to a much brighter life. Now it felt like it was all about to crumble around me...

I just tried to get my head together. Could they write the story even if I denied it? Wayne would think I'd sold the story, and everyone would believe I was just another trashy kiss-and-tell slut, when all I'd wanted to do was the job I was paid for, then leave it there.

Why was I suddenly being asked about this now? Who must have told him? I thought of Jenny. We hadn't exactly got on in the last year, but would she really risk everything for a news story? Maybe she was an even bigger idiot than I thought.

Don't get me wrong, I'm not trying to make out like I'm purer than pure. I've made plenty of mistakes over the years, as you'll read shortly. But I do have my own moral code and idea of what is right and wrong, and for someone to force my hand like this – especially when it was going to massively impact on other people – was just plain wrong.

My son was only five years old at the time. What would he think if other kids at school tried to tease him about his mum and Wayne Rooney? Would he end up hating me for what I'd done? Worse, would social services take my son away from me?

Normally when I'm in the shit, which, let's face it, has happened plenty of times, a plan is already forming in my head, a way to get out of something before it escalates. But this time? Nada. I couldn't strategise to save my life.

Trying to stop my hands from shaking, I rang Michelle, the person I trust most in the world. I couldn't let this ruin me, so I needed to work out what I was going to do. But Michelle, who sees the positive in everything, and usually knows exactly how to bring me back down to planet calm, couldn't find the words. She was as lost as I was.

I hung up and slumped back on the sofa. Without her reassuring words, I couldn't see a way out of this, and really thought I wanted to die. The only way from here seemed to be downwards, and I didn't think I could handle going any lower.

Suicide to me, up until that point in my life, always seemed so damn selfish – surely life can never be that bad, was my thought process. This moment in my adult life was where I changed my thoughts, and soon ended up in a dark hole that I couldn't find my way out of. Death seemed more appealing than facing what was going on around me.

It was only when I thought of my son that I knew I couldn't do it. Thank God is all I'll say on that. I love my life now, and I'm living proof that you can go through just about anything and make it out the other side.

So keep reading, while I tell you the story of my life. I'm not going to tell you not to judge – that would be a bit hypocritical coming from me, given I'm not exactly known for holding back on my opinions – anyone follow me on Twitter?!

But hopefully this story will show you why I became the person I am, in this total man's world we're living in.

Go on, give me a chance … let's turn over a new page.

CHAPTER ONE

P eople always want to ask me the same questions. "Why did you sell your story on Wayne to the newspapers?"

"Who else have you slept with?"

"Why did you actually become a prostitute?"

To answer this last one you need to understand a bit more about where I came from, and what my life was like growing up. Not because I'm trying to blame anyone or anything that happened for how my life turned out. Far from it in fact, I've always been very clear that no one has ever forced me down the path I took, and I've made all my own choices. But it does help explain why I made the decisions I did and became the person I was – and am – today.

So back to where it all began. I was born in Bolton and grew up with my parents, Mary and Steve, and my two older brothers, Gareth and Daniel, in a detached house with a big garden, in a pretty decent part of town. Sounds good so far? Some would say I was very lucky to grow up in the neighbourhood I did, nice houses, surroundings etc, but believe me when I say it, bricks and water mean fuck-all, give me a council house with a family that aren't at war 24/7 any day of the week. We weren't exactly the Waltons – in fact we were probably more like the Mitchells. Because the truth is, it wasn't a happy childhood, and the main reason for that was my dad.

From as far back as I can remember, all that happened in the house, was arguments, lots of screaming and shouting, and things regularly being smashed. My parents never got on, and I never once saw them have a "normal" conversation or be affectionate to each other. The reality was, they'd got married because my mum had fallen pregnant, and with both her and my dad coming from strict Catholic families, it was really their only option. Unfortunately, it turned out to be a match made in hell, not heaven.

Dad was an arrogant chauvinist and was very controlling over mum. She wasn't allowed an opinion on anything, whether it was the way the house was decorated, or the colour of a new car. She even had to do the food shopping off a list Dad would write out, and then pay for it with money he drip-fed her as he thought necessary. She wasn't allowed to look after her own money.

It wasn't just my mum he treated badly, but me too – he simply didn't like me, or at least that was how it felt. I think in the decade I grew up in, parents didn't necessarily tell their kids they loved them that much, which is okay – but to feel unloved, that's totally different, and it's unacceptable and scary.

Mine and my mum's voices weren't valued, were never heard, least of all respected. Being told to be quiet was the norm. My brother, for instance, was going to a nightclub for the first time: I remember this as broad as day, he walked into the kitchen asking if he looked ok, my dad disagreed with his outfit, I spoke up and suggested different colour pants, my dad barked: "Erm, nobody asked you thanks, be quiet!" That was coupled with a look of disgrace that I'd spoken. I was about ten maybe at the time. It didn't make me upset, it did something a lot worse: it made me think this was acceptable. I shut my trap and didn't say anything else.

Some reading this who know me will most likely think I'm talking rubbish, being the big gob I am now. I've always been loud, even as a kid, but as a kid it wasn't acceptable: girls should be seen, not heard. I knew from a young age my dad regretted having me, numerous times I was told I should have been aborted at birth, drowned, that I was a delinquent problem child because I wasn't academically bright. I dreaded homework because I physically couldn't do what was in front of me, but instead of him helping, I'd get a sly crack for being such a dumb arse, sitting at the table staring at work I didn't understand, but I wasn't allowed to leave the table despite the fact I knew I couldn't answer what was in front of me.

Now to a kid that was resilient, that was water off a duck's back, but now I'm older with a kid of my own, I think wow, what a fucked-up pair my parents were.

I still to this day have no idea why they continued to breed, when they obviously detested one another, but I'm kinda glad they did continue, otherwise I wouldn't be here telling you and however many more people my life story, so I think I should thank them for everything!

Sometimes, it would be little things with my dad, for example he was a music teacher and a lecturer, but even though I asked him for years if I could sit down with him and learn to play the piano, he wasn't interested. In fact, he didn't even like me touching it. My dad had a door to his music room that he would lock even if he left the room just to get a drink. That would cause more arguments, as Mum thought that was weird – and rightly so!

Other times though, it was physical rather than mental abuse I suffered (although it's the mental that has stayed with me for longer). Both my parents would hit me when I was little, but mainly my dad. I've always thought a tap on the leg or a clip around the earhole didn't hurt anyone, but we're not talking about a light tap. My dad would take it to the extreme, and I spent most of my childhood flinching around him, not sure what was coming. I remember being five years old, and in my dad's eyes I'd done something wrong. He hit me so hard, he had to keep me off school because he'd given me a black eye – I repeat, I was just five years old.

Everyone in the house would ignore it as though it was normal. I don't know if it was because they were scared of my dad, or because they didn't care.

Me and my brother would argue as kids, just like any other kids did. My brother would never get told off, though, it would always be my fault.

One time we'd been bickering and my dad just walked right over to me and gripped me really hard, then booted me in my left hip, and carried on kicking me time and time again. Every time I tried to get up, I couldn't. He told me to get out the room, but I couldn't walk. A school teacher saw the gigantic bruise on my hip the next day, and still made me do PE. I'd like to think things have changed now, and it would have led to someone looking into it.

To be fair, Dad didn't have the best childhood of his own. He and his two brothers were badly abused from both sets of parents, mentally and physically, while his sisters were strangely put on a pedestal and treated like queens. I personally believe that's why he took it out on me, as though it was revenge for his own childhood, but as far as I'm concerned, while that might be an explanation, it's no excuse.

I'm still waiting for the day somebody knocks on my door and says, "Hi Helen, I'm your real dad." I just don't understand how I'm cut from the same cloth as him, or anyone else in the family for that matter. Everything I want and aspire to be – from my outlook on life to being a very selfless, caring person who loves to look after people and listen to them – is the polar opposite of my dad and my family.

Because of how my dad was, for years I was being really scared of other people's dads. If I went to a friend's house for tea after school and their dad came home from work, or if they were in when we got there, I would sometimes have a panic attack and my mum would have to come and pick me up. People would laugh and say, "You're so weird, why do you do that?" I couldn't really explain it myself. It was something I couldn't control; it was such a bizarre situation. I didn't know at the time that it was actually a panic attack – I just knew I couldn't breathe! I'd see my friends' dads' cars pull up outside the house, and I'd think: "Shit!"

On many occasions, my mum would have to come and pick me up; she would always say "This is ridiculous", and that if it carried on I couldn't go to any of my friends' houses any more, as she was sick of me getting there then having to come and pick me up.

As for my mum, you would think she might have defended me. But she was too wrapped up in her own problems with my dad, and her own anger at the world, to put the energy needed into protecting me. It was the other way around, I started trying to defend my mum against my dad from a young age: finding her sat on the bedroom floor in pieces crying was a regular occurrence. Me and mum weren't ever close, but seeing that hurt me – nobody wants to see their mum cry.

The irony is, she worked at a pre-school when I was young, and was great with the other kids. Yet again, I was asking myself, what had I done wrong?

Being a mum now does naturally make me question why the hell my own mum never defended me? It was a case of turn a blind eye and act like everything's normal. I'm thirty-two now so I've accepted that was part of life, but it's also had a massive knock-on effect with relationships, and having men around my son.

Years later, I met some of my primary school friends' mums at a wedding, and they said they always knew something was wrong with my home life, but didn't know what to do. One of them was in tears even talking about it, but as a kid, I can only remember one of them being a bit more vocal about it.

My oldest friend is a girl called Ashley, who I've been friends with since we were two, and her mum seemed to know exactly what my dad was like deep down, even though she generally didn't feel it was her place to say anything.

But once when I was nine years old I'd been looking forward to Ashley's birthday party all week, but on the day Dad had an argument with my mum, and at the last minute he said, "Helen isn't going to this party, she can stay home." I went into panic mode as I needed to get out the house, and started going a bit crazy: I smashed a mirror in my bedroom and scratched my face, screaming and begging my mum, pleading with her to let me go. Ashley's mum called the house, worried when I didn't turn up at the party, then told my mum that my dad was a bastard for not letting me go.

It's weird, although it's years ago I still remember that shitty entrapment feeling I had inside. It was all mind games, toying with my head and emotions, knowing full well a kid can't do anything. There's no way out. I'd sooner have been beaten black and blue than had the constant head-fucks and endless amount of bloody panicking. I do put a lot of my edgy bizarre ways, how I act now, down to these episodes

The next time I went down to Ashley's house, she called Childline. She was so worried about seeing me upset all the time, and knew I was petrified of my dad, and she didn't know what else to do. I don't really remember what they said to her, but I do remember a few days later she got a letter from ChildLine and handed it to me, and like a dickhead I took it home. Of course, my dad found the letter, and leathered me – a battering for a letter I'd brought home about concerns over him battering me. The irony wasn't lost on me even at that age!

The worse things got at home, the worse my behaviour got at school. I'd start panicking at the thought of being told what to do, and sitting still and concentrating. I'd become obsessed with wanting to annoy my teacher, and couldn't follow the rules. A little devil in my head would be saying, "Sod this, do something naughty," so I'd do something like make a stupid noise, or I'd throw something – anything to be disruptive.

I was stupid because school was a safe haven, my friends have always meant the world to me, so being a tit at school didn't really make sense. I guess that's easy to say now I'm older, but at the time getting into trouble just didn't faze me. Regardless of whether I behaved or not, life at home was bleak, so what was the point in trying to please anyone?

The only time I wanted to do well was when we were doing presentations. I liked getting up to say my piece, so when everyone else would be squirming, "I don't want to go first", I'd be up there like a shot!

I've always been hugely passionate about animals, and once at primary school when all the kids were giving talks on films like Power Rangers or Cars or their family holiday, I walked up to the front, very loud and proud, and said: "Right everyone, I've got a presentation today on where your meat comes from."

The teacher looked less than impressed at the back of the room, but I enjoyed making everyone listen. I'd got loads of books from the library, including a graphic one that I opened up to show the class a pig being slaughtered.

"OK, Helen, that's enough!" said the teacher, but I wasn't going to be stopped.

"Erm, no, you need to know this is where your bacon comes from!"

Still to this day, I get so emotionally drained about what goes on in slaughterhouses, I used to find their numbers in the yellow pages and ring them up from phone boxes calling them bastards. Weird, weird child.

The same teacher put me on report for bad behaviour at one point, and I spent the week being so good to try and make up for it. On the Friday after assembly she asked me to stay behind and I had an absolute panic attack as I really thought I was going to be in more trouble. Turns out she wanted to say how well I'd done, and ask if I wanted the part of Oliver in the school play! All that was running through my mind was the fact the bell had gone ten minutes ago and my dad would be waiting, pissed off because I was late.

I don't think there's any harm in a kid being worried about their parents' reaction if they've been bad at school, but it got to the point where although the teachers were praising me after school when the bell had gone, I was still shitting bricks because I was running late.

It might not come as a surprise after what you've read so far, but at a very young age I started to self-harm quite a lot. Stupid things would come into my mind where I thought I just wanted to die; nothing in particular had to trigger it, it was just the atmosphere at home that I didn't actually understand.

I was the most confused child and I didn't understand why people had kids, because to me I was just always a burden. It was my dad that would make me feel this way. I don't even like saying "my dad", I don't even call him my dad actually – other than writing it in this book, I always call him by his first name.

There isn't any anger or emotion towards this person who was fifty per cent responsible for placing me on the earth. Mine and dad's relationship has always been dire, toxic, aggressive, we weren't meant to be when it comes to parent and child. He did come down to my wavelength though, ONCE, when I was eighteen or nineteen, he randomly came to my house with a box of weed and sparked up a joint – very bizarre, out of the ordinary, he went on to tell me how difficult life had been with my mum and how they'd not been sexually active and she didn't give him what a man needed … hmm, I was like, what exactly am I meant to even say to this?

They'd split up at this point, very noble of him to tell me it wasn't their fault they got divorced (I knew that anyway), so I didn't get why all of a sudden he was trying to get on a level with me, all a bit too late, my head wasn't in it any more, I was sooo done hoping to have just normal fucking parents, they weren't parents, they were two people that detested each other and had kids to try and make things normal, only stayed together because the Church frowned upon divorce, but then bite the bullet after giving their kids the brunt of their shitty arrangement.

I haven't seen my dad in years, I've always regarded myself as a dadless child so it's made no odds. He jogged past me last year while I was out walking the dog, we made eye contact but that's it, there was nothing inside. It was a man I knew years ago, that's all, I don't look at him like he's blood or family.

I was on the phone to my friend at the time and she just couldn't get her head around the fact I didn't say anything to him.

I'm adult now, I could have said something equally, like he could, but say what? Some things are irreversible. I'm a firm believer in the phrase 'life's too short', therefore I don't make any effort with people who aren't going to bring any good, I don't do this whole making up with people who have hurt me in any way, it's a lot easier to stick with people who don't and won't ever damage you, that's my security blanket and that's what enables me to snip the cord quite quick, without the bat of an eyelid when it comes to bad eggs.

More head-fucks from the father. When I was around nine or ten, as I mentioned earlier I love animals, any kind, I feel at peace with them, horses especially. A stables near me where we used to go and walk as a fake family outing, there was a pony being groomed, I went over to stroke it and asked the lady if she ever needed any help, long story short she told me to come down the Saturday after and after I've done a bit of the mucky stuff, I could have a trek on the pony.

We've all been kids, we all know how excited you get in your little minds about the smallest of things. My dad agreed I could do this, which I was shocked at, turns out that was all just for show in front of the kind lady. I worked my arse off that week at school, became a swat, teacher's pet, did all my chores and more at home, I was a golden child, Saturday came, I dived out of bed like a fucking lunatic, got myself dressed and then went in to ask my dad when I could go down...

Then, boom, "I've had a think, I don't want you around animals that big, they're not safe" (but he allows me to be an altar server around priests on my own). Out of the blue, after a week of me being this model child, he completely shattered these visions I'd had for the last seven days, seven days is like a year

18

to a kid mentally, no mention of his change of mind beforehand, he watched me basically arse-lick my way through the week and without any doubt took great pleasure in watching me crumble.

I cried that much I was sick, because I was so hysterical, like most children would be – it then gave him more ammo to punish me even more, for causing a scene. Grounded once again, for what? For fucking what? Can you tell this still angers me to this day? You can't fuck with a little mind like that, it's because of how he was.

I'm SO into the whole insensitive thing when it comes to being a parent. I constantly text my son over any bit of good he does. He loves cars, so if he does well and keeps his head down I book him on a driving course, give him extra pocket money, buy him that t-shirt he's wanted and I've told him he needs to save up for, I'm not saying material things are always the right way, but if a kid doesn't receive some form of praise, whether it be vocal or a gift of some kind, I don't know many that would be the best they can be.

It works for me and my son, anyway.

Running away became the norm, I didn't want to be in that house, I get it that some kids even wanna be grounded, but when a parent is playing tricks with your mind, not allowing you freedom or space for no reason, you begin to go a bit insane. That's exactly how I felt most of my childhood, like I was a freak/mental, the thoughts that went through my head now to this day disturb me.

My mum needed help, some form of counselling, anything to be honest, but was clearly in denial, typical 'bury your head in the sand' tactic. I remember one night I ran out the house because my mum and dad were at war, I couldn't be arsed listening to it anymore, she drove after me with my brother in the car, I refused to get in, we got into a scuffle and she gave up, shouting, "I hope you get raped, you know that!" then slammed the car door and drove off.

My brother will remember that, like both my brothers remember a lot of things, we've just all separated and there's no acknowledgement we're relatives. Looking back, one of my quieter brothers I now feel sorry for, we've spoken about it too, we never will be close, but he opened up about the fact that his childhood has fucked him up badly, that it's had a knock-on effect in his adult life. When we were kids I didn't even know him, he was just a boy that appeared from his room at meal times, that's it. When you're kids, if you're around abnormal things, all the time, it's a routine, you don't see it as abnormal, do you?! But it's only being older I see that he stayed in his room away from the turmoil, whereas I did the opposite and started to lash out.

I despised every single one of them, but shouldn't have. My brothers weren't to blame for anything.

I felt like I was living in a daze, and I never understood what I was doing unless I was at school, where it seemed safe; I kind of just began to exist in this house which should have been my home; I would look at other people's families, and I just wouldn't understand why mine wasn't like that.

I also started to come up with any excuse to spend time with other people in the neighbourhood. I suppose I was lonely. As a kid you don't really tar yourself with that word, it's only looking in from an adult perspective, I know now I was searching for company for a long time.

I think it seemed to be my dad's mission to put hurdles in front of everything – grounding me for no reason, banning me from being around girls like myself, playing out with people my own age etc. – it sounds strange, but I began knocking on other people's doors on the estate when I knew they had dogs. I'd ask if I could take their dog out, just so I could potter about with something, then I'd spend ages talking utter crap to them at the doors when I'd drop the dog off. Looking back, they were probably thinking "I wish this little shit would piss off"!

An old couple lived around the corner and I saw them gardening one day and asked if they needed any help. We got chatting, then next thing you know I was in their house eating biscuits, talking away. I looked at them like they were my friends, and spoke to them in that way too. This became a regular thing, me sitting in their home drinking tea, waffling crap, listening to their stories.

Then one day I was sat with the old lady, she was talking away, and her husband walked in and said, "You here again?" in a jesting-type way. I shrugged and just said yes.

"Why do you keep coming here, what's in it for you?"

I wanted the ground to swallow me up, and my head started racing. Did he think I was a bad kid? Did he think I was trying to rob them? Why does he not like me anymore?

Everything went sour inside of me as he went on. It was said in a light way, but you knew he was being serious – and had every right to be: "Haven't you got your own grandparents' houses you can go to?"

The wife chipped in, "Take no notice, Helen, he's just teasing."

But my heart was pounding, and I felt bloody awful – why was I bothering these people? In my young mind I thought I was some form of help, and I'd nip to the shops for them, help them with bits in the garden, post letters, listen to their stories. So when this got said, I felt so stupid.

I left not long after, and never went round again.

After that I'd always wave, scurrying past, but panicked if I saw them in the garden, I'd turn back around and walk the other way to avoid them. This must've been so odd for them, I get why, I'd be absolutely mortified if I thought for a split second my son had gone to a stranger's house for company. I don't like him pestering the neighbours for a football to be thrown over the fence, so to think of him looking at strangers/ neighbours as some form of comfort would make me seriously question what the hell I'd done wrong.

Quite often as a kid I'd sit in a tree at the bottom of my garden, for ages and ages, take cushions and blankets there, make it some kind of nest for me to chill in, always at the same time of day too. This was a safe haven from home which was only at the top of the lawn, no arguing, no fighting, no being accused of things, just peace, listening to the birds and nothing else.

Cutting and scratching myself were things I did quite often. I think I just picked up how to self-harm, and it soon became the normal thing to do. I suppose it's strange to say I just started cutting myself, but I did. I remember one day I'd been cutting myself in my room and I was sitting on my bedroom floor, looking up at my high bed and thinking I might just hang myself from that bed. I was only about ten years old – and I had no idea where that thought came from. A child has got to get to a pretty low state to think of suicide at such a young age.

I would mostly cut my arms and the top of my legs with razors I'd get from our bathroom. On numerous occasions, I'd have a shower, then cut myself multiple times and just lie there and let it bleed. I'd hit myself and pull my own hair out. It didn't hurt – there were no feelings really, just a sense of release, followed by complete emptiness. It became addictive. Cutting myself started off as impulsive, but it turned into compulsive behaviour. I didn't know at the time that it was probably me coping and expressing my emotional distress. I realise now it was kind of self-help. I think I held so many emotions inside – intense anger, frustration and hurt – and this was a way I learnt to express them.

It silenced the chaos in my house.

My mum found me once in the bathroom straight after I'd used a razor on my legs. She covered it up and I never went to hospital. We never, ever spoke about why I'd done it, instead she went mad, angry at me being stupid and making a mess.

If you're reading this now and find yourself in a similar situation, it can be tempting to cover it up like I did, or to lie about it altogether, but if you're able to share it, it will make a big difference to the way you feel. It will reduce the feelings of shame and isolation and you'll increase your chances of recovering. I know it takes a lot of courage to speak out, but please do.

By now I was going more and more off the rails. I had become part of a popular group of girls that included my then – and now – best mate Michelle.

I wasn't interested in learning anything and I was still naughty, getting detentions all the time, but I didn't mind, as I would be in them with my friends.

I'd do daft shit, like I was once dared to pour zinc and potassium in my science teacher's brew, or put pins and chewing gum on teachers' chairs, all the usual childish pranks that to be honest I've never grown out of!

We'd skip school a lot and hang out in the graveyard for hours. A couple of my friends went through similar stuff to me at home and came from backgrounds where their parents were fucked-up too. It was an escape from our home lives.

One day in year nine we moved things up a gear from weed. It was dinner time and pissing it down, and some scally boys in the year above offered us some Es (ecstasy pills for the more innocent amongst you). It was raining and we were bored. Me, another friend, and this girl called Margot bought some and took her pill straightaway, but me and the other girl thought we'd have our dinner first. (Can't have an E without our chips 'n' cheese.)

We then decided we didn't actually want the E and asked Margot if she wanted to trade in her dinner tickets for our Es and she knocked them both back – I didn't know whether to laugh or panic.

We walked to our next class – IT – and Margot was sat next to me. It was dead quiet and she kept whispering: "Helen, you look Chinese, what's going on?" She was hallucinating and going crazy. Soon she was frothing at the mouth and gurning like mad, but luckily our teacher was a fossil so had no idea what was going on. Everyone in the class was staring at her and I was trying to keep her quiet, until she said, "Helen, my heart's racing, oh shit, it's really racing, feel it." I told the teacher, "I have to go and get Margot a glass of water sir," but he refused, so I ran out anyway as I knew something clearly wasn't right. I got her a bottle of water and came running back in, but she wasn't there. OMG, where was she? Had she collapsed? I thought the worst, but while I was out of the room apparently the head had come in and escorted her out – not because of the drugs but because of something else we'd done earlier in the day: he didn't even know about the intake of class As … yet!

It turned out that someone had grassed Margot up for going through people's pockets in the changing room while they were at PE, so the head of the year had called for her to come for a meeting. Little did he know she was off her head, and had triple-dropped at that... Once they got into his office and sat down he immediately saw something was really wrong with her.

Instead of disciplining her for stealing a few quid he called an ambulance and off she went to hospital and my other friend and I were called in.

The police turned up and kept asking us where we'd got the drugs from, but I was never going to tell them in a million years. I eventually got a caution and was suspended from school for four weeks and then we were off for Easter, so I had six weeks being grounded to look forward to, and a whole lot of hell at home.

Hey, I'm not going to say I didn't deserve grounding, my kid would be grounded for six months on bread and water if he pulled a stunt like this.

My dad went straight to stationery shop Staples and bought me CD-ROMs in English, maths and science; he made me do the exercises all day every day. I wasn't allowed out of the house for six weeks, but obviously I used to sneak out; I was going insane at home. Some of my friends were allowed out until much later than others so I would just sneak out with them, then afterwards I would just sneak back in; I'd climb out my window when everyone went to bed. As soon as I got out I'd leg it and not look back; I didn't think about anything else but getting out of that house. He could hit me later, but right there in the moment after those six weeks I needed out; we didn't have mobile phones then, so when I was gone, I was gone.

It's tough titty on the kids these days. 'Find My iPhone' is ruining the lives of teenagers wanting to stick two fingers up at their parents!

Soon after I was back at school, I got caught with alcohol, and was sent to the behaviour unit in school and had to write lines all day, as well as go on a behaviour improvement scheme during the holidays. We went river-walking as part of the school scheme and on a cigarette break a teacher found weed hidden in my fag packet.

"What are you playing at, after the ecstasy episode?" she asked me. "I'm gonna give you a chance Helen, I'm trusting you to do the right thing, and if not, I lose my job." I threw it away. Thanks Miss, for that extra chance.

Through most of secondary school, I still wasn't interested in boys. It might have been thanks to my home life showing me that a man wasn't exactly something I should be craving to add to my life.

Or, it might be because unfortunately I was sexually abused as a child. A man close to the family had abused me when I was six and seven, on three occasions. The first time anything happened I was sitting in the back of the car on his knee. He started rubbing my tummy and worked his way down into my knickers with his hand; we were waiting for other people to get into the car and I now ask myself why I didn't say anything, but I just didn't think – I was only six or seven. What was I supposed to say or do? I had no idea.

The next time I remember was grim. I'd slept over at a relation's house. I woke up early in the morning, wet through. I thought I'd wet the bed. Panicking, I checked the sheets. But there was nothing under me on the sheets or the duvet. It was just the top of my pants that were wet. I remember there was nothing different down below. I was just wet in that area. I can't actually remember what happened. If I had to guess, I'm presuming he had a wank on me while I was asleep – there's no other explanation.

On the third occasion, he'd sat me on his knee at a relation's house, and I remember I had a tartan skirt on with tights. He had his hand underneath me. He didn't insert his fingers inside me, but he was rubbing me through my tights.

I'm saying this now and you as a reader might be thinking: "Why didn't you say something, Helen?" The answer is, I still don't know. I only told my best friend about four years ago that this had happened. I've never told anyone else until now.

I feel kind of numb to it so I don't know how much it has affected me deep down. I don't know if it has influenced any of my emotions or actions over the years.

I do believe I was targeted, not just because my age meant I was vulnerable, but because I wasn't close to my parents. He knew I wouldn't tell them, and they wouldn't protect me.

This wasn't to be my last negative experience of sexual contact as a child. Looking back I was in awe of older lads, or men. If you aren't getting attention from where you want it the most – at home – you can end up craving any attention you get from older guys, even if they're are giving you it in a perverted way.

I'd done a complete 180 when it came to strange guys being around me, especially older ones. I'd gone from freaking out about their existence to, well, being attracted to them, craving their attention; to me I was this headstrong kid that had everything under control, I was mature for my age or so I thought, you don't see a guy touching you as anything wrong when you've not been looked after in the right way by the right people.

I think that is why losing my virginity was horrendous, and looking back, I can only say that yes, it was rape, even if I didn't fully realise that at the time.

When I was fourteen years old, I was constantly wagging school and going around some of the grotty local pubs getting leathered from all-day drinking – I suppose it was another coping mechanism, I just didn't think of it that way at the time.

This particular weekday we met two twenty-one-year-old guys – twins – and hung out with them for the day. Looking back, they were obviously losers – it was mid-week, mid-afternoon, and they were getting hammered in the local pub with two schoolgirls – we told them our ages right at the start. So not exactly the kind of aspirational man you'd want to be with, really. But we didn't know any better, and sat getting pissed with them as the afternoon went on.

We were having a laugh and when they invited us back to their flat to drink there, we thought why not? In reality, it was two men taking two kids back to their flat: they knew exactly what they were doing.

It's all a bit of a blur after that. The next thing I properly remember is waking up in bed, with my friend bursting into the room, and punching one of the twins who was on top of me naked, having sex with me while I was passed out. He scrambled off and she grabbed our clothes and got me dressed, tugging my jeans up, and rushing me outside to grab a cab.

What the hell had just happened?

The cab took us to her house and we went straight to bed in the attic bedroom; she was still pissed out of her face and I lay there bleeding, thinking, "Shit, I've just lost my virginity and I don't even remember it!" Did he take my pants off? Did I take my pants off? I'll never know. Then as if things couldn't get any worse her parents came in pissed at six a.m., shouting.

My mate went downstairs, where she got slapped about – her

mum had earlier rung the house phone and figured we'd not been in all night so her mum kindly threw me out at six a.m. in the morning with my trusty JD bag, looking like Pete Doherty after a bender; I had to sit at the bus stop for two hours waiting to go home. This morning was a Saturday, so no school: I went straight home and straight into the shower and I just sat there crying my eyes out, hung over. I was hurting and thought: What the hell have I done? They weren't great memories, so it's probably a blessing I only remember snippets. My mum started knocking at the door shouting: "Helen why you are taking so long in there? Hurry up!" I just kept thinking: "Oh my God, he's twenty-one, I'm fourteen, what the hell am I doing?"

At the time I thought it was me in the wrong, whereas now I know it was him.

I felt like shit, I mean I'm sure a lot of teenagers' 'first times' aren't all story-book or movie-like, but I felt dirty. I told my mate never to tell anyone what had happened, I didn't want anyone finding out – especially the school, who might then inform my parents, that's the last thing in the world I needed.

In the shower, I had a love bite on my left swollen bee sting. I remember thinking, "Thank Christ it's there and not on my neck, at least even in this situation there was a silver lining. Sleeping with a twenty-one-year-old when you're fourteen might sound abnormal, but it was a normal occurrence when we were at school, particularly with my group of friends; older guys were the norm to go about with, they paid for things, they made you feel protected to an extent, only later on do you realise this is grooming.

Monday soon came around and we were back at school, I was standing chatting to my mates when everyone started singing

"I got twenty-one seconds to go, I got twenty-one seconds to go." Someone asked me: "Did you shag a twenty-one-year-old, Helen?" I was like, OMG. I wasn't gonna tell anyone about this. I was so pissed-off with my mate as I'd told her not to say anything. I thought I'd be able to have everyone believe I was still a virgin. I try the same trick these days, and people don't seem to believe me – I don't know why...!

I first got caught sticking my fingers down my throat at school by one of the teachers; they brought my dad in, which was just horrific; I begged them not to tell my dad, but they said he could help; I told them over and over: "He won't help, you don't understand." I didn't want him to know, I begged them, but they said they had no choice. My dad arrived, acting all hunky-dory about it as if he was concerned in front of my teacher; I knew it was all an act and deep down he was going to kill me; as soon as we got home he brought the whole family in, including my grandparents; I remember my brother had his friend round too.

My dad pulled a chair out and made me sit on it; while everyone sat around me, he clapped his hands and said: "So today, everyone, Helen's stunt is bulimia; she's now bulimic; is there anything you won't try for attention, Helen?" He was just in my face talking crap, and everyone just stood there staring; no one would ever comment or speak over my dad. I had no bloody idea why my dad called everyone around to the house.

Bulimia is an eating disorder, but I never had any issues with my weight, so to be honest I don't know what possessed me to start with it. I had too much going on in my head for a kid of that age, so maybe this was a way to cope? Who knows.

It became another 'normal' thing for me; I would pull my hair out, cut myself, and now I was making myself sick. It felt like I was completely misunderstood – I still am misunderstood – but being misunderstood at that age, with no one understanding you or why your hormones are all over the place, was a real shit dark place to be. I became even more anxious, but with all these things going on I had no idea what anxiety was, I was just this crazy kid, losing my shit.

I went through crazy cycles in my teenage years where I'd stuff myself with food and get myself up in the middle of the night to be sick; I do wonder if my poor relationship with food comes from my dad too. He had a bit of a strange relationship with food growing up, and he was such a control freak about it; when he was growing up there was a chain on the family fridge and he was never allowed to go into the fridge without permission, but his sisters were allowed a key for it – totally messed-up, I know!

My dad had brought many of his issues from his childhood straight into my life. I ate for comfort really, I'm guessing I was depressed, I just didn't know it: we all react differently when bad things happen; I had no sense of self-worth or self-respect. As a parent, you have a duty to teach your child to respect themselves. If I've drilled anything into my child I hope to God it's for him to know his self-worth and ability.

It's taken years, and I mean years, to realise as I've got older I need to be kinder to my mind and body.

One of my jobs in the house was to clean the kitchen. Dad would always make a point of coming in just to start something with me when I was cleaning: he'd pick a reason out of thin air to be a vicious, narky prick. This particular day he and Mum had World War 464, I as usual got the brunt of it; he was goading me about freedom, which he knew meant everything to me because he knew how much I hated being in the house.

It went from a blazing row with my mum, to me being in the wrong place at the wrong time. I knew I wanted to go out with my grandparents in Rochdale, like school, it was my happy place, so I kept quiet while he tried his best to piss me off. Not biting, he lobs a massive bag of Bombay Mix at the wall of the kitchen. As usual it quickly turned violent out of nowhere, with him belting me, but this time I saw red and hit him back.

I'd had enough.

I pushed him into the cupboard and the door slammed shut on his fingers. Remember, he's a pianist, so he needs his hand to play and teach with; he broke two or three of his fingers, I can't remember exactly, but he had to have them put in a splint for a few weeks. I was constantly reminded every day in the house that it was my fault he'd broken his fingers and we'd all starve to death because his business may fall apart; to be honest, the way both me and my brothers felt living in that house, starving to death may have been a more pleasant option.

I remember as clear as day: I came home from school and got in the shower; I didn't think anything of it, just like you shouldn't; I had my shower, then walked into the front room. My dad came over to me and he felt my shoulder and said: "Have you even had a shower?", to which I replied, "What do you mean? Yes, I've just got out." He said: "Your skin doesn't even feel wet! Go and get back in the shower now!" I just stood there wondering: "What the hell was he talking about? Why would I fake having a shower?" He just started going mental: "There's no way you've had a shower, get back in the bathroom!" So I went and got back in the shower.

Looking back now, I wish I'd just told the prick to get knotted, but I stood in the shower crying, humiliated by the suggestion

I was being unhygienic. I spent a couple of minutes washing my clean body; as I hopped out the shower AGAIN he was waiting outside and told me that I'd been too quick and couldn't have washed myself properly. He then ordered my mum to stand in the bathroom while I had a shower AGAIN. I was crying my eyes out, saying: "Why are you making me do this, Mum?" She was used to this belittlement, but I wasn't; she simply said: "Oh, Helen, just do it."

Having to stand there and wash every inch of my body again for the third time was somewhat of a head-fuck, to say the least. All I can think is, this must be the kind of practice that went on when my dad was growing up.

My dad and mum's family never saw eye to eye, and both me and my brothers would often get caught in the crossfire. My mum and dad had had one of their many arguments, and this particular day we were going out for dinner with our grandparents. I was just excited to be going out of the house and out for dinner with my grandparents; the few happy memories I have are because of my grandma and grandad.

My grandparents did do a lot for us when we were younger. Which I appreciate, as there wasn't really anything else to appreciate had it not been for their input. My grandma turned cold towards me when I left home and then got pregnant. Now when I was younger, I thought, hmmm, yeah she's catholic, it's not her way and all the rest. Then like a lot of things now I'm older, it became clearer how wrong she was. My auntie, my grandma's daughter, is actually her niece, my auntie's mum conceived her around 15 years of age, I think. Not sure how – I believe something seriously fucked up went on, this was Northern Ireland back in the day, so it was rife with lies and protecting bad people, usually priests or nonces in the family.

My grandma raised my aunty as her own, so I never fully understood why I was frowned upon when I got pregnant; was it because I didn't put on a show, hide for nine months and then give my baby away and have everyone believe another person was my son's mum? This was a big secret that my aunt told me when she was pissed when I was 13. She's fucked because of all this, won't admit it and can't stand the sight of me.

But I find I grate on people because they're baffled with how I've carried on solo and how I'm more than happy to tell 'family' to piss off. Too many people in my family on both sides kept quiet over the years about things that aren't meant to be a secret and that's what's resulted in half of them being screwed in the head now. More so than me and that takes some doing.

My grandma would on occasion be at my mum's house and act like I wasn't in the room. This was after all the Rooney stuff came out and I guess she's heard the rumour about one of her favourite Downton Abbey characters and me.

I grew to accept that she didn't want to know, then my son's first holy communion took place. I invited all my grandparents and for the first time in eight or nine years my grandma all of a sudden was happy to speak to me, acknowledge I was in front of her, why? Because a priest was talking to me about my son, praising him. My grandma chirped up, "Yes, I'm his great-grandma and this is my granddaughter, are you coming to the reception father?"

I paused for a second and looked at her as if to say what the actual fuck is going on here? You've not so much as looked at me in the last almost decade, but now a priest's stood here I'm ok to be known. Absolutely hilarious the front some people have.

We never spoke from that day. On my mum's 60th we were out celebrating, and me and my grandma ended up in the bathroom at the same time. She washed her hands looking down at the sink and walked out. I actually stood there laughing, a pitiful laugh. I'm only 32 at the minute but if I ever turned into a hypocrite as big as that I'd feel a failure. My son's going to hopefully one day give me a grandchild, I can hand on heart say I'd not treat anyone I'm meant to love, unconditionally, like that.

One of the final times I saw her before she died last year, she was at my mum's. I was with my son, she didn't bat an eyelid at him, not a hello, not a how are you, nothing. This got on my tits and pushed me too far. She went in the kitchen to hide from us, I'm guessing, my son said bye to my mum and shouted bye to his great-grandma. No reply. He went near the kitchen door and shouted, "Bye grandma" again. No reply. I told him to go out to the car and popped my head around the door. "What you ignoring a kid for you horrible old bitch?" She carried on drying dishes. That's the last contact I had with her.

I didn't see her as my grandma, I saw her as an ignorant hypocritical woman whose morals were fucked. The secrets and lies she'd harboured over the years because she had more loyalty towards a church sickened me. She died. I didn't go to the funeral. Obviously I was slagged off by people that mean nothing, the other extended hypocrites of the family. These same people who couldn't even be bothered to care for my mum the day of the funeral and dropped her off not long after she'd lowered her own mum into the soil.

Mum was in pieces, heartbroken and confused about that day. She wasn't fully aware of what had happened but she knew her mum had gone somewhere and she knows what a funeral is still. It was only on the off chance I nipped round to find her sat without the telly on, still in her black outfit, crying on the couch.

Can you understand why I'm so vulgar about these people when this is what they do? I don't regret not going to the funeral at all, I didn't celebrate her life when she was alive, so why would I mourn her death? She stopped being a grandma to me the day she disowned me but put a show on for a priest a few years later – that was the cherry on the cake.

People say life's too short for fallouts. I totally agree, but I believe life's too short to have to tread on egg shells, too short for fakery, for bad people, to force relationships or friendships; therefore cut the cord and stick with those who are solely good for you. I can't fathom how people make up with people who have shat on them, turned their backs, etc. When you know what you have to offer as a person yourself, it's very easy to leave a unworthy person in the past where they belong.

Which brings me back to when my dad, in the rage of an argument, threw the massive bag of Bombay Mix at the kitchen wall, and he said, "You (meaning me) can clear that up before you go anywhere." I immediately went into panic mode. "Why do I have to clean it up, Mum? Please help me. Why has he done that?" My mum went to help me, and he ordered her to stop.

She did, and left me to it. Now for a start-off, if someone did that to my child they'd be six foot under, but my mum was more concerned about what time the table was booked for, and the family moaning at her because she'd be late. So she got in the car with my brothers and left me at home clearing up his mess. Again, yes, it was just a pub lunch I was missing out on – but to a child…! I just literally felt dead inside.

I remember sitting with my back against the cupboard, with

a dust pan and brush and the doorbell going. I actually thought, "Thank God, she's come back." My dad closed the kitchen door so I couldn't get out, and then opened the front door, but it was one of his pupils coming over for a lesson. He greeted them with a big, "Hello, come in please", like everything was 'normal' at this house.

There's no word other than empty to describe how I felt at that moment – or any other moment in that hell hole.

Only one teacher noticed something wasn't quite right with me. She was the head of discipline, and had a reputation equivalent of Miss Trunchbull – the headmistress of the school in Roald Dahl's Matilda. But she always looked out for me, and told me, instead of lashing out in class, to just come and take a breather in her room.

I'd go to her room where she'd be working, and I'd hang out and have a brew. One day she decided to call my dad and ask him in for a meeting.

He came alone and was absolutely furious that my teacher had insinuated that my behaviour was to do with something going on at home. I don't know exactly what he said in their meeting, but my teacher had to call someone to come down and get him removed from the school premises.

Clearly, he hadn't been interested in trying to work out what was wrong with me – he was just about protecting himself.

After that, the teacher brought social services in. I didn't really understand who social services were, but I started to see a counsellor called Bill who used to come in voluntarily and I would go to him twice a week out of my lessons. He listened to everything I had to say, and I really enjoyed the chats. He was the first man in my life to sit down and say, "Helen, you're going to be okay." He understood me, and I liked him, and hearing about his daughters and granddaughters. It made me happy to hear what a good family life could be like, even if I wasn't experiencing it for myself.

By then my dad was refusing to give me dinner money because he said: "You're bulimic, you don't need any."

So instead, kind Bill would give me dinner money and tell me to go and get some chips or something I wanted.

After a year of seeing Bill my dad found out he was giving me lunch money and banned me from seeing him. My dad took the one positive male influence in my life away from me. But what did I expect? It felt like he ruined everything that was good in my life.

CHAPTER TWO

With no Bill to chat to, I was at absolute breaking point, and started to run away from home all the time, even if I just went to hang out in a country park for the night. Although I was still only fifteen, I dreamt of being able to get away and set up life by myself.

My friend Emily said I could stay at hers for two weeks; but her mum reported me to social services.

I was adamant I wasn't going home this time, so they started looking for a place for me.

"So, Helen, you're going to stay with a lovely couple. They're a vicar and a deputy head teacher, and you'll be their first foster child."

"Are you shitting me?" I was furious. Unless I was moving to Craggy Island with Father Ted and Mrs Doyle, there was no way I was moving into some God-squad gaff. Then again, what could be worse than living with my dad?

I arrived at my foster parents' house all cocky and defensive, but I didn't need to be: they were amazing people. I was their first foster child, and they were lenient with me as they were learning the ropes and the boundaries. I was only supposed go to them for a few days, but I stayed a few months; I felt safe there and I loved the freedom. Social services gave me a curfew, but I was a teenager and I didn't really give a shit; they did make me feel really comfortable and welcome, and it was so much better than living at home.

I totally abused the fact this amazing couple hadn't fostered before: I'd get ready for school and leave with them to head for the bus stop, then go back home when I knew the coast was clear. Going less into school was becoming the norm, as I could easily get away with it. I'd met my son's dad by this point, so began to sneak him in and we'd spend the day in bed.

Andrea, my contact point in social services, was really lovely to me, and I'm still really good friends with her to this day. On one occasion, when she visited I thought she was just coming to check up on me, but she had bigger news.

"So, Helen, just to let you know, your parents have signed you off into permanent care." Now I know most kids would be crying, devastated, but I was absolutely delighted about it. My parents were happy to ship me out as I was coming up to my sixteenth birthday: I was just three months off it. Andrea said: "You have two choices now, Helen, you can live with another family nearby, or you're entitled to your own flat." I immediately said: "Own flat!" Bloody hell, a place I could call my own home, yes, that's exactly what I wanted…

Days after my sixteenth birthday, I was given the keys to my flat. I was so excited, although it wasn't quite the cute place I had imagined. There were loads of smackheads hanging around all the time: it was a dreadful one-bed flat, no furniture, no washing machine, it's surreal to think of it now. I had to wash my school uniform over the bath tub, but I was buzzing at first, as it was the first place that was just for me. Peace.

The flat was vile, damp and freezing, and although my neighbours were smackheads, I had an older lad living above me who was a gem, he'd often check up on me and let me know I could ask him for help if I ever needed it, nothing sinister in it.

I was a bit sad when I left my foster home, as they had taken care of me, and did really kind things like taking me to Ikea to buy me stuff for my new place. They did question me again and again, asking me if it was the right decision, but I'd made my mind up I wanted my own place.

By this point, I had been dating James for a few months. It seemed to be going well, and I liked his parents, who were really chilled. He was coming to stay loads in my new place, and we were having fun. However, I started feeling really lethargic for a few days on the run, and living on my own I didn't actually mention it to anyone. I thought maybe I was burning the candle at both ends; it wasn't until I collapsed in the flat that I knew I needed to go to the doctor's. My boyfriend's dad took me to the hospital and they said I had a PID, a pelvic inflammatory infection caused by an STD, a sexually transmitted disease.

I was sent straight home after the tests and put on medication but my cramp was so painful, it wasn't going away even after a few days with antibiotics. I lay in my little flat crying, for a week; after that I couldn't take much more, so I went back to the hospital and they ran further tests, which is when they said: "Helen, we've found something else." All I thought was, "Oh, shit, I'm dying, what have I caught?" They said: "The results have come back, Helen, and you're pregnant." I was sitting in the clinic on my own, and I'd just been told I was having a baby.

Oh, My God!

They carried on speaking, telling me I didn't need to decide right away on anything, but I couldn't speak. I didn't say a word. I was in total shock. I just sat there in silence, taking in that I was going to have a baby. I went back to my boyfriend's after the hospital and told him, then lay in bed, where I stayed for a few days; we were both in shock; I couldn't take it in; I didn't want to be alone in my flat. He wasn't happy at all, and said: "Helen, what do you want to do?"

"I don't believe in abortions," I said. There was no doubt I was keeping this baby.

We sat down and told his mum; she'd always been really nice to me, and caring; she had guessed something was going on, and it crossed her mind I was pregnant. I knew I was keeping the baby from the moment I found out. I was just so quiet, as I had to get used to it, it was a lot to take in.

I went back to my flat and carried on going to school, but I had the worst morning sickness ever; everyone at school knew, all the teachers and all my mates. I wasn't the first, though: one of my friends was also pregnant; she left and went to a specialist baby unit, whereas I stayed at school; I was going through my GCSEs, and didn't want to leave.

My friends were great while I was pregnant: every single day I would get on the bus and Michelle would be stood in the aisle commanding everyone to put their fags out the window: "Helen's on now!" she'd shout, and they would all do as she said. She would also bring a bottle of water and an apple for me every day; she knew I was being violently sick all the time, and I was struggling to look after myself; she was like my angel.

As the pregnancy went on and got harder, and as I got more and more tired, I stopped getting up for school altogether; Michelle, bless her, would come and get me up every day; she'd let herself into the flat, open the curtains and be like: "Come on, get ya-self up!" I'd be like: "I'm not comin'", but she'd drag me slowly out of bed and feed me the water, apples and yogurts she'd brought with her, and she'd more or less carry me to the school gate.

I hadn't spoken to my parents in months, they hadn't checked on me, or asked to visit. So I don't know why, but I rang my mum from a phone box to tell her I was pregnant.

"I don't know what you want me to say," she said.

I don't know what I had expected, but I guess I wanted to reach out to her at that point. That a bit of me knew I was going to be a mum, and it would have been nice to have my own mum around.

I don't blame my mum for a second, she was a shit mother, but she was so wrapped up in a miserable existence she couldn't function properly; there was so much crap going on in her life that it was like she couldn't hear me.

A few days later my dad got hold of me.

"Right, your mum's told me what's gone on; how far are you?"

"Ten weeks."

"Well, erm, we need to think about this."

"Who's this 'we'? There's nothing to think about."

"Well, actually, there is, Helen."

"There's fucking not! I've made my mind up this baby is mine, and I'm having it!"

He was like a dog with a bone, going on and on, but all he was really arsed about was his kid having a bad reputation for being a pregnant teenager, and what on earth would he look like to other people.

This life inside me was mine. I had never had anything of my own, nothing that I loved, and there was no way I wasn't going to guard it with my life.

My dad called again a few days later to tell me he'd had a discussion with my grandparents. Well, I knew which way that was going to go – they're Bible-bashing weirdos, who didn't give a shit about me. Strict Catholics are the most immoral people on earth to me, and religion should be banned as far as I'm concerned, it does nothing but cause hurt and lies; if you're offended by this, I don't care.

So Dad continued: "We've had a chat, and if you want to terminate the pregnancy we'd be happy to tell everyone you'd miscarried."

I lost it. "What the actual fuck are you on about? Are you deaf? I'm keeping the baby, I want this baby, it's mine! Besides, why are you bothered? I'm not coming home, I'll go to college, I'll get a job."

So I got on with the rest of my pregnancy by myself. I was still with James, but he didn't move in, in fact he was going out drinking all the time, while I spent most of my time alone and pregnant.

To make matters worse, his grandad passed away and this messed with his head. One day, soon after he'd passed away, I was out shopping and James was in town drinking; he called me and said to come and meet him in the pub, so I did; I wasn't drinking as I was pregnant, and I hadn't been there long when he started gobbing off at me; he got thrown out of the pub for shouting abuse, so we started walking home to my flat. He was in a foul mood, saying horrible things to me and hurling abuse, real nasty shit like "I hate you, you've ruined my life, I wish you'd died instead of my grandad."

I was like "What? What is going through your head?"

James kept saying, "You've ruined everything." Then: bang! He kicked the shit out of me in the middle of the street.

I was seven months pregnant and he was throwing punches and hitting me hard, throwing me around like a rag doll. I was screaming as he kept punching me and kicking me and dragging me around in the street.

It seemed to last forever but it was probably minutes, then he threw my house keys at my face. I was shaking, and said, "Please, just go home and stop this, I'm pregnant, stop it now!" He came closer, right up to my face, and threw the keys again, this time over a fence; I sat on the floor crying, then he ran off.

Once James had left, a female taxi driver got out of her car and came over to me. "Are you ok? I've just seen everything." I was shocked she hadn't stepped in to help, but then I realised she was crying and I understood she was scared. She climbed over the fence for me and got my keys and took me back to my flat, which I'm grateful for. My eye was busted and I had a fat lip; I got into bed, crying my eyes out, until I eventually fell asleep.

The next day his mum rang me and said, "Where are ya?" I said, "At home, why?"

It turned out his mum had been in the Co-op, and the taxi driver happened to be in there. She pulled his mum to one side and said, "You ought to know what your son did last night: he kicked the shit out of this pregnant girl – it was horrific; you need to see if she's alright."

His mum was crying, saying repeatedly: "Oh, Helen, what's he done to ya?"

I didn't really know what to say and what could she do, give him a slap around his legs and ground him?

I didn't tell anyone what had happened. All my friends already hated James and said he was a bad egg. So I became a recluse. I'd sit at home all day for the last three months of my pregnancy; I couldn't afford to dress myself; I looked like Michael Jackson on his most bleached day ever; I was obviously depressed – I didn't realise that at the time, and my mates were getting on with their lives. I'd just sit there alone, I was so anaemic, so drained, and I'd watch stupid boring holiday programmes or Cash In The Attic, then I'd sleep for hours on end. I was living on boxes of Jaffa cakes, they were my addiction.

Looking back, I was lonely. A lot of women will relate to this, being in similar situations, although a baby is inside you and it actually comforted me – it's the most comfort you could ever need. I just got on with it, and my only exercise was to walk to the Co-op to get more Jaffa cakes.

All the days just blended into one. On the one day I did drag myself down to the shop I happened to notice an advert in the Co-op window: "£5 Kittens For Sale." Now, as I've told you, I'm obsessed with all animals; I don't know what made me do this, but I bought a kitten; I called him Bob; I went out for Jaffa cakes and came back with Bob. I loved Bob so much: my little black and white cat; he kept me company; deep down I think I knew he would be my little companion, and it was getting lonely being pregnant and living on my own. He was my little mate in that hell hole of a flat.

At seven months, the council gave me a new home. Not much nicer than the last, but it was a bit bigger. I was still with James, despite his behaviour, but we were on an off, as going on the piss with his mates was his priority.

Then, at eight months pregnant, I went into labour.

I was in M & S, shopping. I used to go in there all the time because if I wasn't eating Jaffa cakes it was an M & S cauliflower grill, which I still love to this day! (I highly recommend it; if the food buyer at M & S is by any chance reading this, you can send me the grills in copious amounts, ta very much.)

It was 1.30 p.m., lunchtime, and I felt a twinge. I took a deep breath, and at this point I just thought: "Ah, it's just a pain, maybe I need a big fart", and I went home. I carried on with my day as much as I could; I was doing the dishes in my Winnie the Pooh nightie, looking a bit like Vicky Pollard with long hair, when Emmerdale came on, and then, bang! A massive contraction at seven p.m.

I thought, I can't be in labour, it's a month early. Who did I call? After no contact since finding out I was pregnant, once again, it was my mum who I wanted to speak to.

"Mum, I've gone into labour, I know I have."

"No you haven't, Helen, it'll be Braxton Hicks; don't worry, it won't be a real contraction."

"Mum, it's not, I can't get comfy."

I curled up on the bed for the evening, but the pain was getting worse and more frequent, so I called my mum again.

"I'm in agony."

Again she told me to hold out, but at one a.m. she agreed to come and take me to the hospital.

At the house James told her: "Helen's upstairs, lying on the bed." He was just sitting there playing on his PlayStation like on a normal evening.

My mum drove me to the hospital, and when I arrived they said they were going to give me an internal. I'd never had one before and didn't know what to expect, which I think might have been best. I had no idea how sore it would be. I squeezed my mum's hand so tight I felt like I was gonna snap her knuckles.

They finished the internal and gave me some diamorphine. I was all over the place, drifting in and out of sleep; I started talking about my brothers and my dad; I was hallucinating and I kept saying I wanted to see my brothers and my dad, I repeated it a few times and my mum must have called home. My dad came down; I had no idea if I really wanted him there or what I'd been saying, he just stood with the door half open with his head around it, and said "How's it going?" What did he want me to say? Well, I've seen better days; I've got a head fucking partially flopping out my kipper, what did he expect? Did he want me to stand up and do the river dance for him? He just stood there and left again before I'd even given birth; he said something like, "Well, I've got to go and teach", and off he popped.

I was in labour nineteen hours, which can be normal for the first birth; when my son was born he was making a little noise, which at first we thought was cute; the doctors, however, needed to take a closer look; they found he had mucus on his lungs so they took him away to the neo-natal unit; I didn't think he'd be there for long but he stayed for two weeks; he was poorly, bless him. They kept me on the ward, but I discharged myself in the end; I couldn't sleep and I felt like shit with all these other babies on the ward; it was driving me mad, listening to them cry but not being able to hold my baby. Every night, though, I went to sit with my son and, granted I was a sixteen-year-old girl, still in the sixth form, but I tell you what, those nurses couldn't have been nicer to me; they'd give me a chair and a blanket and sit me in a quiet corner and let me hold my son and talk to him, night after night.

CHAPTER THREE

Taking my son home for the first time was exciting and scary, but I was determined to do my best.

I was so adamant to make this a success right from when my son was born, even though I was sure everyone thought I was gonna be a shit mum and mess it up.

I'm not saying I was the world's best mum because I wasn't, but I did everything properly so no one could pick fault with me.

I was quite lonely at first, as it was just the two of us most of the time. My mum adored my son, but Dad and his family stopped her coming over as much as she wanted to. They said: "Helen has made her bed, leave her to it, you're doing her a favour not getting involved."

The one ongoing problem was my boyfriend. My son had still been in neo-natal when, two days after he was born, his dad went out "wetting the baby's head" and a fight broke out which tragically resulted in one his best friends being killed by a police car. James's mental state got worse and worse from there, and his behaviour to me deteriorated rapidly. He would be out drinking every night, and then come home and take it all out on me.

A mate and I were at my house one night, about three months after I'd had my boy, when James came back home pissed. He started hurling abuse at me and goading me, getting louder and louder. My friend knew which way it was gonna go; she went upstairs and got my son in his snow suit and ran straight out the front door. He'd started beating me up by now, and head-butted me so I fell back on to the bedpost, which snapped. I landed on the underneath of my armpit, which by now was gushing blood. I eventually got out and ran down some back streets after my mate.

It was one-thirty a.m. in the morning and freezing cold; we ended up on a petrol station forecourt and we rang my dad and told him we needed help. Eventually he came and got us, but barely said a word in the car and just dropped me outside James's mum's house, and he drove off.

She opened the door and was gobsmacked. She couldn't believe what was happening. I ended up sleeping on the floor with my new-born baby that night: it was all so wrong, but at least she was there for me – no way could you say blood was thicker than water when it came to the Woods household. Anyway, James left a lovely scar to remind me of him.

You'd think after this that I'd grow some balls, move on, and stop associating myself with James, but no, this was only the start of two crap years. Luckily my son doesn't remember anything, but that atmosphere spoilt what was meant to be a precious time when you've got a child.

It became the norm for James to sleep at different houses, mine always being the one chosen when he was most wasted. The nights mostly ended badly, but the one that sticks with me the most was more about humiliation than physical pain.

It was a typical start – I was making food, asked him if he wanted lunch for the next day, he muttered something, pissed, I barked at him to speak up, and then ... well, he pushed a fridge on top of me. A jar of jam had smashed on the floor at the same time, and he got my face and rubbed it in the jam, and then stood there laughing at me. I tried to wipe the jam off but he kept rubbing my face back in it. I got up and I was crying my eyes out. I could hear my son crying in the cot upstairs, and James walked out of the house, as he'd done many times after beating me up.

I thought he'd gone and was sitting with my back against the cooker, wishing this was just a nightmare, and contemplating what the hell I was doing with my life (I do this a lot, you might notice), when BANG! All of a sudden he appeared at the kitchen window, thumping it with his fist, and shouted loudly: "Boo!"

I was terrified and on edge, then he came back in the house and went for round two, and started hitting me all over again.

Out of every single kick, punch and scar, it was having my face rubbed in the jam and crying at him shouting "Boo" that I found most harrowing out of everything. I'll never get over that level of humiliation. I couldn't even kick him out of my house, as he'd just turn up whenever he wanted to. His relationship with his son was non-existent from the beginning; he would say, "Shut that baby up, it's annoying me." He didn't really acknowledge him. Even when I said enough is enough and I want nothing to do with you, he would kick the door off.

I didn't ring the police on him, although maybe I should have. But even though the neighbours did a couple of times, the law was different then, and if you didn't press charges yourself, nothing happened.

But then one night I was out at a place called Jaxx where everyone used to go. I was chatting to a lad from school, all innocent, believe it or not, when out of nowhere I was head-butted in the side of my face. Surprise, surprise, it was my James. I saw red, grew a set of balls, and finally retaliated. I punched him back, I had a bottle in my hand that I smashed in his face. I wanted to kill him at this point, and got pleasure out of seeing the shock on his face, which was covered with blood. It took four bouncers to get me off him, then the police came and put him in the police van; I went outside to watch and he started crying, saying, "Look what you've done." I started laughing, and in one last swipe I threw the only shoe I had left at him. All a bit EastEnders-ish I know, believe me, my toes are curling I was ever involved in these scenarios.

You might wonder why I didn't get arrested – I do too! – but I think people saw he'd gone for me first, and also the police knew what I'd been going through with him.

I felt brilliant watching him locked in that van, but the feeling didn't last. His mum was devastated – again – and told me he could go into the army if I didn't press charges. So the next day I dropped them, and hoped that talks of the army became a reality.

I was still calling all my mates to come over whenever they could, as I wanted company. My friend Tanya, who had a little girl, came over one night. We were watching a film when James turned up yet again. He'd been at the pub all night and when I refused to let him in he kicked the front door right off and marched into the house.

I swear with him I had more callouts for new doors than I did for Domino's.

Tanya's baby started crying, and Tanya called a cab straightaway; she could see what state and mood he was in, and she just wanted to get out of there. She was waiting for the taxi when things got heated and he head-butted me again, this time while I was holding my son, in fact he head-butted me so hard I nearly dropped my baby. Tanya was really crying by now, and panicking, trying to get out of there. To top it all off, her baby was physically shaking; I went and put my son upstairs, but Tanya's baby looked like she was having a panic attack.

I can't believe I'm saying this now, and obviously my friend's baby had never witnessed anything loud, scary or violent before. I've never seen a baby so petrified; it's the saddest thing, and it breaks my heart to think about it.

Her taxi arrived soon after, thank God, and she said to me as she left: "If you ever even look at him again, let alone speak to him, I'll never see you or be your friend; look what he's done to my daughter." And she left.

I went upstairs to check on my son and he was just sat there like it was a normal day in our household; he had a toy wheel on his cot which he was playing with; he'd got so used to hearing these noises, he didn't even look scared. This is when I spoke to the police again; I got an injunction this time, but his mum begged me over and over again not to press charges. I understood she was his mum, and I thought it over and decided to let it go.

Over the next few months he got arrested over fourteen times; I had my injunction but that meant nothing to him, he just kept coming back and kicking the door off.

Eventually, as my son turned two his dad finally went into the army; I didn't see him for years and there was no other man in my life other than my baby boy. I'd had enough for now.

Around this time I decided it was time to get a job. I needed out of the house, and some focus, and a way to earn money.

My first job was in retail, and hands up, I've got to say I was pretty shit at it! I hated every single moment, and spent my shifts eating butties, stuffed behind shoe boxes in the stock rooms, and hiding behind rails whenever customers came in. I'd make up the craziest excuses not to go in, getting more and more extreme, until I even told my boss my son's dad had kidnapped him.

I got a new woman boss, who slapped my arse in the stock room, which I didn't take too kindly to. Had that been a fit male, slap all day (I say this humorously in case I offend any snowflakes), but the real deal breaker was when she listed new rules and said I wasn't allowed bottles of water or chewing gum on the shop floor. Me and stupid rules don't go well together. My time in retail was over.

Next I started work in a call centre. I was a general dogsbody but I was happy to be that, as they plied us with free food day in day out, let us finish early, and rarely checked what any of us were doing. This, my friends, was my idea of heaven ... then I got moved to a room miles away from everyone. I was with an accountant who was the sweetest lady ever, I actually did some work here, she kept me busy and because I liked her I was eager to impress her, so I finally started to show signs of work ethic, which hadn't been seen since my paper round or when I sold PVC underwear on the market ... yes, that was a real job!

My next role was a bit of a change of direction – I became a lap dancer. But did I do any better there than in retail or a call centre? No! I was the worst worker there...

I'd like to take this moment to take my hat off to these birds that graft their arses off, because it's so hard to do. I was terrible at getting clients in, talking to some stinking bastard with sprout breath with a tenner to his name, no thanks; I'd walk around like a pissed giraffe in daft heels; I'm not a high-heels kinda girl at all, pass me some wellies or a nice pair of flip flops and I'll moonwalk with happiness. It has to be the hardest job, working from eight p.m. to six a.m., getting home and then having to take my son to pre-school. I'd put my son to bed and go and work lap-dancing while a friend babysat, and I'd be back in time for him waking up. It paid the bills, so I stayed there for some time even though it was a miserable existence.

Around this time on a night out, I saw a girl being horrible to a school friend's younger sister, goading her for no reason. I walked across the bar and asked her: "What's your problem with Rachel?"

"Why? Who the fuck are you?" she barked at me.

I gripped her neck, pushed her over the bar and slapped her. Probably not the best thing to do, as I got barred from the venue, but I'm always going to defend my mates.

Anyway, it turned out this girl was called Jenny Thompson, and she was soon to play a much bigger role in my life. If only I had trusted my initial impressions from that night that she wasn't a good egg...

Three months later she was in a bar every Dick and his dog went to; I hadn't noticed her until she came into the toilets and asked if she could have a word with me; I told her to piss off and she just asked me to hear her out; we had a chat for about an hour in the toilets, standard female toilet practice; I felt for her, not straightaway, but I knew she wasn't this person she made herself out to be; she cracked inside and broke the sour surface. My feelings towards her did a 180 and we became really good mates over a period of time, we'd spend quite a bit of time together and I thought she was a really nice girl; we'd always have girly chats.

There was some form of mutual understanding between us; although we didn't talk about things at first when we became pals, I knew she was pretty fucked in the head, as was I, so that was the common ground. The worst foundation any relationship can grow on, basically.

By this point I was working in the lap-dancing bar four days a week while holding down yet another new office job. I sat there all day on the phone, pretending I had a clue what I was doing. I was like David Brent – all the gear and no idea.

Naturally, trying to hold down the two jobs, I was knackered, and doing a useless job, so it wasn't long until it went tits up and I was fired.

This is all my own doing by the way, I'm not pointing the finger or expecting an orchestra of tiny violins, but it was a kick in the stomach. I needed cash.

CHAPTER FOUR

I had rent due, and loans to pay off – what was I meant to do? I went home and put Magic FM on so I could listen to sad songs, and sat there on the sofa with the Kleenex and cried. It was a proper 'woe is me' moment – eat your heart out Bridget Jones – but I couldn't understand why all the shit kept happening to me.

Jenny was texting me, asking about plans for the weekend, so I rang her. "I can't do anything, I've lost my job, I'm bolloxed."

"Why don't you do what I'm doing?" she immediately said, and told me she was working as an escort.

"What do you actually do?" I replied, intrigued. "Do you just go out for something to eat, or do you have to shag them as well?"

"Some guys just want to talk, but most of them want to have sex with you. But it's easy, and dead good money. You've done lap-dancing, it's like that except you aren't going to be in front of loads of people."

I thought for a minute, but the idea all seemed a bit seedy. "I don't think I could actually shag them."

"Well, think about it, babe," she said, and hung up.

While we were talking I'd moved off the sofa and was now in front of the TV. With a start, I realised my face was just inches from the screen, as I stared at it mindlessly like an idiot, without taking it in.

I didn't like lap-dancing as I didn't like prancing about with everything on show in front of the other girls. I also couldn't stand the gawping men who were looking at me free of charge, before they decided if they wanted a dance or not. So, I had to admit this would be more private...

The only time I'd come across escorting was on Belle de Jour, the TV drama with Billie Piper. Thinking about how she got paid to have loads of kinky sex, I started to think it didn't seem that bad after all. In fact, I realised I had worked worse jobs plenty of times.

Maybe I needed to be decisive, and go for a big change in my life? It's not like things had worked out great so far, so was it really that bad to take this risk?

I could clear a bit of debt, and look for another job at the same time. I'd be out of there in a month and no one would know. (Yeah right, that'll be the biggest lie I've ever told myself then...).

So yeah, there you go, it was as simple as that. When people ask me why I got into brassing, it was a pretty straightforward need for money. No one forced me to do it. I was handed a solution to my problems, thought about it, and decided to go for it. Being a prostitute was straight up a choice of my own.

Before I could change my mind, I rang Jenny back. "I'm in. What do I need to do?"

The very next day I went with Jenny to this gated, luxury two-bedroom apartment in Worsley, Manchester, to meet the owner of the escorting agency. For some reason I didn't feel nervous, just more curious about what was going to happen.

Melissa came in all glam, head to toe in designer gear, and surprisingly young. I'd been expecting a Bet Lynch kind of woman to walk in, leopard-print fur coat, no knickers, and a 'show us what you've got' kind of bitch-type figure!

She asked me some basic questions, but all the time I could tell she was assessing my looks and personality, and making sure I wasn't a drug addict. There are plenty of negative things I could say about Melissa, who fancied herself as a bit of a poor man's Alan Sugar, but while a bit of coke was ok, she wouldn't have ever had anyone there who was heavy into drugs.

Eventually she told me I could make loads of money, and

I would do really well. She called me an 'elite escort'. Quite funny that, isn't it? Not once was I rewarded at home or in school, but the day I became a brass I was told I was 'elite'!

Melissa explained I would be paid directly by the clients, and then I was to give her twenty per cent of what I took. I thought it was weird she didn't collect the money and then pay me, but I found out later it had to be that way around legally, otherwise it would be classed as pimping.

Most of the jobs would be done in the apartment, which I was happy with, as it was a nice place, and felt safe, but sometimes I would be expected to go to the guys, in hotels, or in their homes.

Just a few minutes after we had agreed on everything, Melissa said, "Right there's a guy coming right now, do you wanna see him and get started?" I laughed: "Yeah, bring it on, there's no time like the present!"

I didn't feel shy or afraid at all. In fact the only thoughts that went through my head were that luckily I'd shaved my legs that day, and I had matching underwear on.

I walked downstairs into the room, then this average-looking Italian guy in his thirties followed me in. He didn't speak great English, but he put the cash on the sideboard. Looking back I've now idea why or how, but for whatever reason I wasn't nervous and I suddenly took charge.

The only thing was, it was like it wasn't really me, I had snapped into a different person, and fallen into a kind of character. This weird voice came out of nowhere: "So, babe, have you had a nice day? What can I do for you?"

It was like I was in a dream and my normal mind had gone numb, and this other person had taken over. I may as well have been working a job in a factory. I was that unbothered about what I was about to have to do, I just kind of went through the motions, acting like I'd done this job for years. And then, like that, it was over.

I had a second job in my first afternoon, an outcall at the Midland Hotel, Manchester. We had drivers who would take us to the different locations, and wait there until we were ready to leave. Again, I just fell into my role. It wasn't until I got home that evening that actual Helen re-emerged. I felt disgusting, and ran to my bathroom and scrubbed myself clean for ages in the shower. That's it, no more, I thought. That job was not for me.

But then I did the maths and realised how much of my debt I had cleared in just a few hours' work. The weight on my shoulders lightened a bit. If I stuck it out just a bit more, I would have it cleared in no time. Sod it, there was no way that was going to be the end of it.

Before long, it began to feel like a regular job to me – and one that paid really well, with minimum hours. It didn't take me long to realise that it's actually quite an addictive job for the life that it can give you.

I would mainly see guys during the day. This helped me maintain some normality as a mother, working nine to five. My driver would pick me up and take me to the jobs. I soon had loads of regulars; they would take me to nice hotels, some would also buy me presents, which I was never bothered about, in fact it would make me feel slightly uncomfortable: being bought stuff is not my thing (unless it's food, give me a three-course meal over a pair of shoes or a bottle of bubbly any day of the week); in day-to-day life I look after myself.

I think my need to be financially independent is because of the control my dad took over finances with my mum. I don't need any guy getting a kick out of being in control of my money and possessions, I can look after myself. I wouldn't say no to sharing a life with someone, but someone dictating and managing my money, absolute no go.

Really quickly I built up my work persona, working under a different name that I'd taken out of a pretty racy book I was reading at the time.

Then everything else, well ... I just made up as I went along. I said I was from Chorley and had no children. The further I could make it from the truth, the less chance I thought there was of anyone ever finding me outside of work, or happening to mention me to someone who knew me. I loved putting on an accent, as it was great craic between me and the girls I was working with, and even if the men thought I was taking the piss, acting the clown made the days pass quicker.

I built up a bit of a routine to how I had sex. It sounds awful really, kind of robotic, but that was how you got through it, and it seemed to tick the boxes for the clients!

Mostly I would sit on top of them, kiss round their face and their ears, and talk dirty, telling them what I would do to them. Then I would start playing with their cock, and try and get them as turned on as possible before they were actually in me, so that the sex was over as quickly as possible.

Most of the time I would be saying something like: "I want you to fuck me as hard as you can." When really in my head I would be thinking: "I wish I was watching Come Dine With Me with a pie and mash and a glass of wine!"

It might sound brutal, but they all knew deep down that they were paying for an act, and I just acted well most of the time.

I need to stress here, men who use escorts/brasses aren't bad, horrible, dirty people, there's reasons as to why we have men paying for sex, from just being horny to having major issues with self-esteem, so it's an escape mechanism.

The actual chat was another big thing for me. Some of these punters were genuinely interesting people and they liked a conversation and how I responded to them like a friend... I could also chat a glass eye to sleep, so talking away meant they'd need to spend more. As you feed a guy the attention the desire builds, if you can show interest and be interesting, before you know it, they weren't booking in for a half hour, but are there for two or three hours. That way they weren't rushed and could talk. When you think sex lasted mostly between eight to twelve minutes, getting a salary for three hours for it wasn't bad.

If they really liked you, they would ask you to stay. This scenario was perfect for me. I'd tip my driver who was waiting, he'd tell the agency he had dropped me off back at home after an hour, then I'd keep the money and not have to pay them a fee. I'm not usually a rip-off merchant, but that industry is slightly different. I kept the agency sweet, sticking to days as promised, but I'd keep a handful of clients to myself once I trusted them ninety-nine per cent.

My clients were a total mix. For whatever reason the older guys used to prefer me, and I preferred them. The oldest one was maybe in his late fifties. They were always very straightforward and sweet, and were very admiring of your body. I would often leave those ones on a high, having been made to feel good about myself.

A lot of the time these men were in unhappy marriages, but didn't want to have affairs because of their profile, or they didn't want to risk getting caught out and ending up with a divorce, because of the issues it would cause with money or kids.

I didn't like the younger guys so much. As a general rule, any guy under the age of twenty-five would treat you like a piece of meat.

The only younger ones I liked were the virgins. They would come in like Jim off American Pie, with no confidence in themselves, wanting to know how to please a girl so that they were prepared for sex in the real world, whenever it came along – one day!

I really enjoyed giving them lessons, like that's too fast, or that's going to irritate a girl, this will work better. They could ask anything they liked and I would give them all sorts of tricks. I thought it was quite sweet of them really to want to get it right, and not just be thinking about their own pleasure. Although time and again the biggest mistake most of them made, where I had to correct them, was "Don't drill a girl into the mattress!"

One of the most memorable was the youngest lad who ever hired me. He was seventeen, and he booked me at his house while his parents were away.

He answered the door, and was so, so nervous. He told me: "I saw you on the website weeks ago, and I've been putting money away ever since, to pay for tonight."

Then he went and brought his rabbit out. Not the kind of rabbit I would have preferred, but a real-life fluffy bunny. He sat telling me all about how she chewed through the TV cables, and I could see she was just like this scared, cute kid. If he'd been an idiot, I would have let him chat on and waste his money, but as I liked him, I went and put my fingers on his lips to shush him, then took control. As it turned out, he could have taught some experienced men a thing or two. Hopefully he's making someone enjoy a sex life that's worth writing home about – and is no longer using bunnies as a way to chat up the birds!

I had many punters who all wanted different weird shit, like one guy who always wanted to call me his dead wife's name and have me act out how she would perform sex on him. I had auburn hair at the time, which he later told me his wife had. He started to get too personal like I was his actual girlfriend, and I had to pull the plug on it.

On a few occasions though, things have taken a darker turn and I think I have only got out ok as I'm good at trusting my gut instinct.

One evening I was at a flat and the guy's vibe just didn't feel right. There was something a bit manic and off-key about him, and I decided I wanted out.

"I need to leave, I don't feel well," I said.

"What's wrong with you?" he demanded, as I packed my stuff up.

"I'm sorry, I don't need any money."

He grabbed my arm and pulled me into the kitchen. "You need something to eat, that's what it is."

Normally I might try and be cocky to get out of there, but there was something about this guy that made me think he was a weirdo, right on the edge. I raised my voice. "I want to leave. Let me go, and I'll come back next week, I promise."

I started saying anything that I thought would get me out of there. But he wasn't having it, and started trying to kiss me.

I pushed him away and started getting louder: "Get off me!"

He panicked and pulled me back in, biting my face. I pushed harder and rushed out, just as police were arriving in the car park. I guess we were louder than I realised. Of course, when they asked if I was ok, I nodded and ran off. I could hardly ask for their help, given my job.

On another evening, I went to a quiet apartment block near Manchester United's grounds, and the guy had the phone to his ear as he answered the door. He didn't speak to me, but waved me on through to the bedroom, really dismissively. Instantly I was on edge. I listened at the door and heard him say, "She's just got here now."

That's not information people normally share, and I just knew something wasn't right. I bolted out and just ran, ringing the driver as I went. As I ran around the corner a car spun in, with two guys in the front. I'm sure they were coming to the house for me.

My friend's dad used to drink in the same pub as us, and in conversation one evening described a certain man, and said, "If you ever end up in a room with him, you leave straight away. He's an evil bastard." He didn't know about my work – he was talking more about at parties.

But sure enough a few months later me and another girl got booked for a job at the Hilton, in Manchester. There were three guys in the room, and the second we got there, I shit myself, as I knew one of them was the 'evil bastard'.

We went to the bathroom to get ready, and I told the other girl: "This isn't a good situation. He's from near me, and I've heard loads of bad stuff he's done to girls."

The other girl was pretty mouthy, and said: "I'm not arsed, I'll tell him what's what."

I was worried she would make things worse, and said: "No, whatever he says goes, he's evil. Just keep your mouth shut."

Taking a deep breath, we headed out – straight into the

middle of a row. He was arguing with the others, and began smashing the room up, pulling things off the wall, and ripping the curtains down. One of the others nodded at the money and said: "Just get off."

We got off as fast as we could. Christ knows what might have happened, but it was one of the few times I've felt someone was looking down on me and keeping me safe in that job...

I don't mean to make them all sound like psychopaths though, because they weren't! I've just told you the more extreme stories, the ones that keep people entertained in the pub. The reality was, the majority were normal guys, who if anything treated me with more respect than I'd received from men elsewhere in my life.

Some regulars had my number, but totally respected that when I wasn't at work I wasn't at work; the number was there to book and that was it, no cheesy shit or lovey-dovey texts, just book and fuck. One of my favourite clients – yes, I did have my favourites – who I was seeing for some time, would contact me directly and ask me to go to his house a lot.

Sex was always good with him – he was like the ultimate fuck buddy, hilarious, knew what to do with his piece, and he looked like Gerard Butler – and then I got paid, BINGO.

It went wrong one night though, thanks to my wig... I would always wear a clip-on fringe, fake ponytail, or wig with all clients, partly to complete the look, and partly to make me less instantly recognisable if I ever saw them out and about.

This night, I'd gone for the wig option, with my own hair tucked inside an awful-looking stocking underneath it. But it didn't matter what it looked like, as no one would see under the wig, right? Wrong. This guy was banging away at me from behind, when he decided to pull my hair. Jesus Christ, not the mullet! Luckily it didn't fully come off, but I told him to get off me and said I needed a wee; I ran off to the toilet to sort myself out because my Anthea-Turner-crossed-with-Rod-Stewart wig was hanging on by a thread...

He came into the bathroom while I was trying to lodge my second head back in place and although he was obviously shocked, bless him, he was polite enough not to say anything, but to leave me to it. I came downstairs with wig intact and said I needed to leave.

I was shocked by how embarrassed I was, as normally I would be the first to laugh off something like that. It could only mean one thing – I liked him. There was no way I could let my emotions get caught up in my job.

I thought about it some more. Looking back, I don't know why I disguised myself with him. I know even if we lived next door, he wouldn't have dropped me in it. But at the same time, ninety-nine per cent of clients talk to you like they want you to be their girlfriend. It's just an in-the-moment thing and I'd laugh and shrug it off, but I realised I couldn't have reacted like that with this guy. So that was it, I never saw him again. That was the best thing I could have done. The worst thing a working girl can do is imagine these guys have genuine respect for them, because they don't. Whether you find that out then, or ten years down the line, it's an unfortunate fact.

Business mind needs to dominate over emotion.

CHAPTER FIVE

One of my favourite clients was a dairy farmer; didn't feel like a job whatsoever. Happened to be hung like one of his Friesians too, so that was a bonus. Yes he was married, but he's one of a few men I felt sorry for, his marriage was a sham. He'd met a 'lady' in Wilmslow, they dated, got pregnant, things moved fast, marriage, baby, moving. Then she turned into a nightmare.

Now I'm only getting his side, of course, but I'd say I'm quite good at judging a character. He was super sweet. If he was any more relaxed he'd have been in a coma, so I couldn't grasp why he had such a bitch for a wife. They had two babies, which they conceived through the odd shag. She refused to sleep with him and they had separate bedrooms. Her bedroom connected to the side of the house where her kids slept, he was on the other side. It was a really fucked up set up.

He didn't slag her off, he didn't call her names, he joked about how he was like one of his bulls – used for his semen then left to one side. He thought he had a problem with sex, simply because he wanted to do it more than three or four times a year. Now although he's married, he said he was never going to leave and she wouldn't leave him, but he's pretty sure she entertains elsewhere.

I used to visit him whilst the kids stayed with family and she went on "holiday with friends". Naturally, I wanted to push for more info and I really wanted to shake him and say wake the fuck up, but the guy was so accepting of this life, this sexless boring life.

The house was unreal, absolutely stunning, we took full advantage of every room, except the wife's, of course. I asked a few times if we could go in the hay bales but he never took me on. It was all cosy nights in with wine and plenty of sex. After we fucked he'd lie there with his hands on his face, obviously guilty. That usually sets in once they've cum, but I'd change the conversation.

I don't think he should have felt guilty; he had a wife that didn't work, wouldn't date her husband but she could go away for countless weekends with 'friends' knowing as a farmer, it's not exactly a job you can get cover for. He loved his babies and loved her too, I just don't think he was in love. When I started to see my ex, I called it a day from seeing him; one of the few clients I really did miss and often wondered if he was ok. I hope he is.

Sportsmen are probably the number one punters in the escorting world as they've got everything, but to some it's not enough. Sex is a big thing, men love sex, and if they can pay for a girl who's really flirty, they will. What's the worst that can happen? Wife finds out? They never leave anyway.

Jenny and I regularly worked together and I liked getting jobs with her as they were easy and fun. We were in Liverpool one night at the Radisson hotel, making our way up to a client's room, but as we got in the lift, the door opened and a well-known British boxer was already in there with two of his trainers. They were about to get out when the boxer asked where we were going. When we said we were going upstairs they stayed in the lift with us and went back up. The boxer said: "Come for a drink with us?" But Jenny told them we were working.

"Working doing what?" Jenny told them we were escorts. I'm sure they knew it from the minute we stepped in the lift to be honest. They told us to sack our booking off and go with them to their room. I'd already been iffy about the job as the guy had been very demanding and particular, asking us to wear a secretary's outfit when he booked us, so it was a no-brainer – we went with the boxer and his friends.

We got into their room and sat down, chilling together. Then it was agreed by the trainer that himself and his boxer mate would stay together with Jenny and I would go with the other trainer, then we'd swap an hour later.

So me and this guy went next door and just lay on one of the beds and chatted. He said he wanted to meet me another time instead of paying for sex, and take me out. He was a really nice guy offering to do a nice thing, not just taking his pants off and demanding sex. I liked him and we got on, but I acted like I didn't want to know. Deep down I didn't know how to act around nice guys, and I'd get embarrassed. I wanted them to treat me like they were paying me, as I guess it was all I knew. It was easier.

The hour was up so we walked back in and the trainer continued to fuck Jenny: he pummelled the shit out of her, her hair was like a cave woman's, her arse was redder than a baboon's. The boxer just sat there in the corner and wanked himself off while his watched his trainer pound away; they'd switched roles: he was the spectator for once.

Afterwards, both the boxer and his trainer then showed us pictures of a holiday they'd just been on with their kids and wives on their phones, and asked about our lives. As usual I lied about everything, and couldn't understand how these people would stand there and tell you the truth about their lives. The boxer handed me the money and I split it. I can't remember the exact amount, but Jenny and I headed down and had a drink on our own at the bar and then left. I've never seen them again since that night, although I kept in touch with the manager for a while, until he got a partner.

I started seeing an ex-Man United player as a client occasionally. He was married with kids, but every time she was away with the kids, he would book girls to come around. I always found it weird, as it was like he wanted to respect it as his marital home, and not have sex in the bed he shared with his wife – so instead he would set up a load of mattresses in the kids' play room to shag on. Ok, because that's much better...

He wasn't English, and had no interest in talking – it was all wham, bam, thank you mam, then you're done and on your way. Some girls see that as an easy client, I actually found it harder to deal with.

That wasn't the weirdest part though – that bit involved his agent. Every time I was around his agent would be there too, and while this footballer was shagging me, he'd be kissing his agent at the same time and they'd be spanking each other. Who knows if he was bisexual, in denial, just a bit kinky ... but it was very bizarre.

He was soon to be replaced in my phone by another Manchester United player, though...

Jenny and I were on one of our nights out in Manchester, in the Living Room – a bar where any typical girl our age used to hang out. We were downstairs, drinking, when one of the staff came over and said: "There's a private party upstairs, do you want to go up?" So we headed upstairs to the private room for a nose, and it turned out it was a Man United party.

Forget the players, and the fact I was on a night out, I was starving. Shock, Helen thinks with her stomach again! But I can't just go out and not eat, and suddenly there it was, like a mirage – an untouched buffet. All the other girls in the room were dying to eat (penis), yet here I was, sniffing out the vol-au-vents. I left Jenny at the end and side-walked like a crab along the bar until I reached the food, and began devouring the prawn toast. Unfortunately, I failed to realise sesame seeds and lip gloss don't mix well.

Jenny had grabbed us some drinks and we headed to the toilet, bumping into Cristiano Ronaldo on the way, who stopped, stared at me, and burst out laughing.

Eh? Why was this cheeky sod taking the piss out of me?

We got into the toilets and I was like, what just happened?

"What the fuck, Helen, you've got food all over your face!" Jenny said to me, half laughing, half disgusted. "You might have just ballsed up our first client!"

After sorting my mush out we headed out and I saw Wayne Rooney outside, smoking. We got talking and he came across as a normal down-to-earth guy, really approachable, not at all pervy, and just spoke to us about normal mundane shit. Then he asked if we fancied going to the casino, where the majority of the mob were.

We explained we were meant to meet up with a different Man U player from the group later on, and told him who. He laughed and said: "Well, he's not gonna be happy, is he?"

"He's a dick, so I'm not too fussed what he thinks," I replied.

Quietly, I made it clear to Jenny: if anything was happening we were getting paid, I didn't give a shit who they were, in fact the hourly rate was going up in my head.

I saw it that you charged, no matter who the person was, whereas Jenny was quite happy to fuck footballers and famous people for free. While her mum was cooking downstairs in their house she had a threesome with two actors from British TV shows. Another time she shooed me and my son out of the house when a footballer arrived. As much as I think Jenny is a horrible slut who is out to get whatever she can, she was brought up in this suburban mansion in Bolton, where her parents were fully aware of what and who she was doing, but because they were famous, it was ok.

I've had a couple of friends over the years who have been born into families who encourage their daughters to gold dig, seek fame, teach them working is too good for them, etc. If you tell them they're owed the world by a man, a girl will learn to believe and live by that, until nobody actually wants them.

We arrived at the casino, which was chaos: the players were acting like total dicks, chucking food everywhere; in particular Wes Brown, Rio Ferdinand and some others were chucking bacon butties and even furniture around, and the poor waiters were just having to tolerate it and pick it up like you would do with a toddler. I don't care how pissed they were, they were behaving like animals.

They were living up to the stereotype of footballers – too much money , no idea what to do with it, and obviously getting a kick out of watching people clear up after them – wankers.

Let's face it, even £80,000 a week can't buy you manners, people skills, or a personality!

We started talking to Wayne again at the bar, who told us that this was normal behaviour.

He suggested a fag and we ended up in the disabled toilets with him and his brother. There was a little bit of flirting but nothing to write home about, it was just general chat.

But Rio clearly thought something more was going on that he wanted to be involved with, and began banging on the door, effing and blinding. "Come on girls, what's going on in there? Let me in."

Wayne was laughing and saying: "Ignore him, he's just pissed." But eventually he had to open the door before it got broken, and we just pushed out, past Rio.

It was getting rowdier in the casino and to be honest they were all doing my head in, apart from Wayne. The version of him we saw that night was just a normal bloke, not a show-off twat like the rest of his team-mates, and he seemed okay considering the rest of them were off on one. Having said that, despite nothing actually happening that night, you can just tell, and we kind of knew we'd boxed a job off with Wayne. Jenny gave her number to him and she took his down, but then we headed home that night alone in the car.

A week later we were sat in Jenny's kitchen when Wayne messaged, asking what we were doing, what had we been up to, general chit-chat. They had a bit of a conversation that ended with them sorting for us all to meet up.

On the arranged date in August 2008, Jenny and I went buying new underwear together for his benefit, then went for something to eat at San Carlos in Manchester; he told us he'd message us when he was ready. It was around two p.m. in the afternoon on a weekday when he texted and said he was ready, so we left the restaurant and headed over to see him. To me it was nothing out of the ordinary, he was just another client. He told us which hotel he was in and we went straight up to his room and knocked on his door. It didn't feel like anything different to my usual jobs, really. People always ask questions like, "What did you feel when you met him?" and I say: "He's a human with a cock, like every second person in this fucking world, it's not anything spectacular." There's nothing to be star-struck about when you meet a footballer, I just saw him as any other boy.

To be honest I was assessing him more as a client, and in that way he seemed he would be a good one. Respectful and well-off, so I was thinking he would make a good regular on the quiet. There was never any thought in my brain to play God with his life or try and fuck him over. One hundred per cent for the record, never, ever. As a reader, if you want to believe that, it's up to you.

He answered in a white fluffy robe and slippers and we went in and we just sat talking for a while. I can't quite explain why, but for some reason I think he instantly regretted booking us from the moment he opened the door. I'm not sure whether he genuinely didn't want to go through with it, or if it was a lack of sexual confidence, but I just got that feeling.

It's a shame he just didn't have the same balls that he has on the pitch, and say that he just didn't want to do it, and he could have changed his mind. But he didn't, so we got on with things.

Jenny and I got changed in the bathroom, just like most jobs, then we came out and went over to him lying on the bed.

Now, given I know we weren't his first, I was shocked by just how, well, bland, the sex was.

He wanted to go on top first, then we swapped around and I went on top of him and Jenny was sat on his face.

We played around with him for a while, Jenny went down on me and was kissing me while he just watched and said in a really monotone voice: "That looks nice."

Nice! You know someone has literally nothing to say when they use that word. An ice cream is nice. A chocolate fudge cake is nice...

I might have thought Wayne just wasn't into us, but other girls have said they had similar experiences with him. It seems he's just very shy about sex, and there was so little sexual emotion in him. Looking back afterwards, I put all his lack of confidence down to the fact that he got with his wife far too young, when he should have been shagging around freely. Maybe he'd know about loyalty and what to do with his dick if he'd got with her much later on.

Whatever the reason, it was turning out how I imagine a couple to shag when they've lived together for fifty years. The sort that eat the same pie and chips every day for tea, but feel they need to do the deed to class themselves as a couple.

Even when me and Jenny were sucking his cock he just lay there like a cabbage.

When he came I was sitting on top, and didn't even realise, until I noticed he'd gone floppy.

"Have you come or something?" I asked, and he said, "Yeah, I came a bit ago", but he hadn't given any indication. I climbed off and headed for a shower.

The thing is, you may be reading this thinking, "You're a couple of brasses, no wonder he's not putting some welly in," but a few friends who I worked with over the years have slept with him, allegedly – you'd think there might be more to him. There used to be an 'arranged' limo ride and canal ride on the Manchester canal where footballers would get brasses, and it was one big orgy. I never participated in anything like these, though, and sex parties were never my thing – being passed around like a blow-up doll I felt was different than being used on a one-to-one basis.

We were in his room for about an hour and a half.

He went really quiet when we'd finished. As I was putting my smalls back on I asked if he was okay, and he said, "Yeah", then paused. "Why have I just done that?" I said, "Well, why did you do it, then? You don't need to worry, just forget you've done it, I'm not going to say anything."

"You can't say anything," he replied, smirking. "You'll get hurt if you do."

He started laughing, but it really pissed me off: "Eh, what's that supposed to mean? I've got just as much to lose as you, so don't start with that."

He said about Coleen being pregnant, and I said: "I've got a son myself, I'm hardly going to ruin his life for the sake of a fling, am I?"

Wayne was one of the first clients I mentioned having a child to, but it really got my back up that he thought I might have an ulterior motive, and I wanted him to see how serious I was. It felt like we were singing from the same hymn sheet and maybe it put his mind at ease, as that's when he showed us the scan picture of his first unborn child. I acted interested, like you do when people show you these things, but when you're on a job it's different. I don't want to know the truth about people's lives, and I don't want them to know about mine. Sex and money, yes. Family trees, no.

Wayne put our money, around £1,200 for each of us, in the bathroom cabinet, and told us to get it from there. I prefer that, actually, than collecting it in my hand.

I said again, before we left, "Just to be clear, don't worry about it."

But I could only speak for me. It seemed Jenny was plotting for something different all along, and she said, giggling, "I've already told the paps."

"Fuck off," Wayne told her, while I gave her a look: "Shut up, you dick."

I had no intentions to screw that guy over. I wasn't going to tell anyone, and I don't even think he would have told any of his mates.

Jenny and I got in the lift and I said, "Jenny, you can't tell anyone about this, it will literally ruin our lives." She swore she wouldn't; but it was really bizarre. I'd just been naked in bed with this girl, but within seconds of getting in the lift, deep down, before she'd even started making sly calls to the press, I knew that was bullshit, and my relationship with her was done. I subconsciously drifted away from her from that moment.

Turns out Wayne's feelings of regret didn't last that long, as a week later he was going somewhere in Europe for a football tournament, and texted Jenny saying, "Can you two get here in the next couple of days."

As it happens, it didn't work out, and things went quiet from him again.

As far as I was concerned, unless Wayne got in touch with us to hire us again, that was it. Job done, get on with the rest of my life.

But it wasn't like that for Jenny. Instead, she started claiming she was having an affair with him. I didn't believe a word she was saying, as I'd seen him shit himself at what she'd said that first day, so there's no way he would have taken the risk.

There was an escort who Wayne regularly saw, who used to pose as a cleaner with a couple of other girls and go round to footballers' houses, or a hired house, and see them there. She was engaged and had a baby, so naturally wanted to keep things quiet – she was, I suppose, the better kind of working girl. I told her about what had happened and that I was worried about Jenny's intentions, and she warned Wayne off her.

It wasn't long before Jenny spat her dummy out, as she didn't like being ignored. This is what began to piss Jenny off, instead of just leaving it be, she began to chip away at him: "I'll get Wayne to sort it" became her go-to, for a short period of time, which then turned out to be what I can only describe as blackmail; didn't take long before she was demanding regular drop-offs of money and free shopping trips to Flannels, a shop in Manchester, to keep Wayne sweet. I'd imagine at this point in his life he was shitting himself daily. She began texting him constantly, asking him to buy her things – she just didn't leave him alone.

She would ask for designer items from Flannels. Wayne knew the owners and he would pay for things and she would go and pick them up. She even picked money up as well. He got lads to drive to Manchester for her and give her money on at least three occasions that I remember, giving her around a couple of grand a time.

I think he could sense from what she said in the room that he needed to keep her happy, but I couldn't stand that shit she was pulling. If I could blackmail every single guy that did the dirty on me I'd be able to buy myself a whole new identity and a new island to hide away on. But I had no intention of fucking mine or this guy's life up – there was only one pit viper with that plan.

I told Michelle about it, and she said "Helen, you should go and meet Wayne again, put it all on a piece of paper and leave your number, and just warn him not to bother with her. She's gonna grass you up." But I never got the chance to see him again.

Jenny was so cocky about the whole thing as well, thinking she'd got one over on him. That's when we started to get bitter towards each other, because I was like, "What are you doing?" I couldn't stand it. It also got me thinking – if she was going to blackmail him while he had a pregnant wife, what could she do to me?

She began acting like a bunny-boiler wannabe WAG, and started getting really angry because she didn't see him again. He obviously didn't want to, with the way she'd been treating him, I mean, who needs that shit?

My relationship with Jenny was giving me the worst anxiety. Do I keep her sweet, do I beg her again to keep quiet, do I leave her be until maybe the novelty wears off? I was shitting myself, really – who knew what she was thinking, or what she was going to do? For the two or three months after the Wayne job, I gave her a wide berth, and made out I needed time on my own away from the job. In reality I was still working, but was doing jobs independently, away from the agency.

Then, just as I thought it might have died down and things moved on, I got a text off Jenny inviting me back to a house party she was at, with a load of our mutual friends. I'd just been out in Manchester, so thought sod it, and headed over. Looking back, I genuinely think she set the scenario up, knowing how it would go down.

The house was packed when I arrived and everyone was getting on it. I walked into the kitchen and the first person I see is a guy I know called Nigel. He walked over to me in front of everyone, high-fived me, and gave me a hug. I had no idea what the big deal was, until he announced: "Yes, Helen! What about you and Rooney, eh?"

The whole kitchen heard, including Jenny, who was stood there. I stared at her across the room and she knew I was so angry.

"Can I have a word please?" I said. She knew what it was about, and fobbed me off, knowing I wasn't going to make a scene about it.

But I was really pissed off by this point, and grabbing her arm, I said in her ear: "Go to the front door now."

Much as Jenny thinks she's a tough nut to crack, I think she knew at this point I was ready to stick her head through the window.

We stood in the porch, and she asked: "Babe, what's the problem?"

My eyes were watering, I was shaking, I was so angry, and I said to her, "I'll murder you if any press come for me because of you. If anyone comes for me, I will kill you." She said, "You need to chill out, babe, they aren't gonna say anything."

We never spoke for about nine months after this; I got in a cab and left, and realised I had to cut her out of my life for the long term, not just the short term: she was bad news I didn't need. I'd had enough of licking this girl's arse, treading on egg shells, constantly worried that she was going to screw me over. Regardless of how I treated her she had every intention of setting out to ruin lives. I wasn't prepared to hang about and watch, I just waited instead.

The footballer world is pretty sickening and I know we can't tar every footballer with the same brush and some who I've met in the past are nice really ordinary guys.

Over the years I've learnt so much about what a status like that and money can cover up; even worse certain WAGs play along with these scandals. Journalists are well aware of numerous footballers that have got girls pregnant, some even being teenagers, abortions to follow, along with the life-long contracts or money flow that keep families quiet. Whilst the money talks, superinjunctions will always stop these stories from getting out.

It's no skin off my nose, but it's still very confusing why there's one rule for a man with money, yet if a woman behaved in that way, whether rich or poor, they're less likely to be protected. Like myself, for instance; I fucked up and live a life sentence for doing so, yet some men can shag anything with a pulse, rape, impregnate girls behind their wives backs and all the rest and still be granted anonymity. Tell me this isn't a man's world and I'd bloody laugh.

CHAPTER SIX

I was still doing my escorting, but all independently now, away from the old agency, and away from Jenny. All I wanted was to get on with my job, earn the cash, and live a quiet life without people talking about me. I decided I needed to put some extra distance between my personal life and my work, so I started working in Ireland. At that point, that's where the money was at, as working in the UK wasn't very good: Eastern European girls were taking over, and worked for a lot less. I would fly over to Dublin for about six days a month and do three days in one area, and three in another. I didn't want to do anything that left a trace, and I trusted this woman that I worked with in Ireland.

My clients in Ireland were the same kind of people as in the UK, and soon enough I started to build up a base of regulars.

I used to see a Dublin judge about once a month. We never actually had sex, but he liked to chat. He was open about his job in the courts, and told me he slept in a single bed and hadn't had sex with his wife once since their kids had left home. It seemed that his wife thought that sex was just to reproduce, not for fun. "I was used!" he would joke. "I was a breeding machine and now I'm no longer useful." It was a story I heard surprisingly often from client: wives who got no pleasure from sex, but saw it literally as a means to an end – children. I felt sorry for these women, missing out on all the pleasure they could have got in the bedroom, either because they had been brought up to believe it wasn't right, or they were scared, or whatever. But I also felt sorry for the men, who did know what they wanted, and were now tied for life to someone who wouldn't give it to them.

Just like I'd seen with my own parents, religion and the bollocks that came along with it, particularly in the Catholic Church, had a lot to answer for, in the crap sex lives of so many people in Ireland!

Anyway, this judge always had these weird requests for me. One time he turned up with a holdall bag.

"Guess what's in the bag."

"I have literally no idea."

"Ok, put these on, then you can feel it."

He passed me some Jimmy Choo shoes and these hideous see-through stockings.

All I could feel in the bag was a box, then eventually he told me to open it up. I opened it slowly to find... would you believe it... a vegetable steamer. I was chuckling to myself but also trying to remain composed.

"Do you want your meat and two veg steaming?" I couldn't stop giggling. "What do you want me to do with that? If you want your veg steaming today, that's extra!"

But nope, he was perfectly serious. He had it all planned out.

He lay on the floor with his eyes level with the steamer, and asked me to stand all over it and crush the steamer. Not his vegetables, like other men might have asked, but the actual bloody steamer. Then at the end I was to put my shoe through the lid and swing it on the end of my heel. Can you believe it, he was rubbing himself throughout, and came off that.

Judge Steamer had creamed his vegetables!

I couldn't help it, I just stood there laughing while he got embarrassed and said: "We won't talk about that again."

But you know what, I wasn't bothered. If that's what floats his boat, then I'm fine with it. If you aren't hurting anyone else, I don't care what people do for kicks.

I could see a lot of men were thinking sex was a bad thing, like they were committing some kind of sin – some were, obviously, but some I feel thought sex was dirty, wrong to do, a guilty pleasure, when it's not.

One thing I've found over time is that a lot of men, particularly men in powerful positions, like violence in sex directed at them – not just GBH against vegetable steamers!

Whether it's because they spend all day having to take charge and make the decisions, or because it's normally them who gets to push people around and they get a kick out of the reverse, I've no idea. But nine times out of ten, if a request came in for someone to be dominated, kicked, whipped or whatever, you knew they had a high-powered job.

I found domination easy to do, as sex was rarely actually involved. If I had a boring client or a really shit day, a client like this would make it so much better – course I don't mind choking some daft sod out with his own belt. If that's what he wants, that's what he gets.

One night we had a booking come up in Galway and it was a request for a "domineering girl".

He wanted me to boot him in his ribs and bollocks. I put a belt around his neck and dragged him out of the room and outside onto the balcony, and made him sit there like a dog! I kept moving his chin with my heels and then I ate half a crumpet and threw it on the floor for him to fetch and eat my scraps. This guy was loving every minute of the experience, but to be honest I wouldn't even do this to my own dog – I would report someone if I saw them treat an animal like this. But for me this was easy money, I got to laugh with my work friends, and got paid without lifting a finger … just a whip.

One regular client who likewise never wanted actual sex, he just loved being belittled. He'd come early in the morning before work, around eight, and act like a dog. I'd pull him around on a leash; both myself and my friend would watch morning TV while bouncing pieces of toast off his head. He loved having my foot under his chin, I'm calling him all the names under the sun, I'd call him a pathetic little wanker and tell him to kiss my friend's feet, all this while we're drinking our brews. Nuts.

Put the shoe on the other foot though, and it wasn't so much my thing. I was up for most sexual requests, but the client dominating or demoralising me was not a job I'd take. I liked being in control of the situations.

I had one guy who booked me at his hotel, and it was such an odd experience. I walked into this room to find him holding a briefcase, but not just any old case, it was full of wallpaper paste. He filled the bath with the paste and wanted me to splash around in it. I got in and everything, but I was sat there like a moody child. I did laugh a bit too, but all I was thinking was that I wanted to smash this guy's head in; it wasn't my kind of thing at all. He kept saying, "Just splash around in it for me," and told me to put it on my tits and rub it over myself. Eventually I just got out of this bath and told him, "I'm getting out now, if you need some help papering your chimney breast you can pay me to do that, but you can fuck this right off."

There was another guy I saw, only once thank God, who had empty bird cages in his house but not one bird in sight; huh, normal?? They were all around his room and they freaked me out; he also had loads of chairs all around his bed with lots of mirrors tied to the chairs, it was really bizarre. He wanted me to lie there on the bed and he wanked while looking at me. I had to get in all these different positions, rolling around the bed; now, I'm not the most angelic of creatures so when I try to look sexy, I should look like a minx, but I probably looked like someone doing their first attempt at break dancing: it was hard to look sexy, rolling around for ages on my own.

Call me boring, but I prefer to have sex in a missionary position than piss around on mattresses like I'd been spiked with spice. I swear this guy was just so strange, he was like a serial killer. In fact I reckon that's what had happened to all his budgies...

A Scottish guy booked myself and one of my friends I worked with a lot. I was in a stupid mood that night, both me and her used to bounce off each other, no pun intended there, she was getting ready in the room with this poor guy, who it turned out was a virgin, and I came through to the bedroom; I was in a really stupid mood, I couldn't go from "Helen" to "escort", so naturally I was being my immature piss-taking self; I swung open the bedroom door and put on a high-pitched Glaswegian accent: "Hellooow, my name's William Wallace, what brings you here today, my wee friend?" He was a virgin, no idea why he booked two girls, bless his heart, but at least his breaking-in was memorable.

My friend burst out laughing; he looked horrified; we got talking, and my Glaswegian accent continued; this poor sod was asking me the most stupid stiff questions: he asked me how long I'd been doing this for? I replied, "I was only a wee lassie when I started, I was kept at the bottom of the garden in a shed and I felt there was no way out, and then I discovered you filthy wee bastards would put some money in my pockets." I'm laughing at this point, he's nervously laughing, then just to top the whole weird scenario off, my friend was laughing that hard she farted. I left the room and let the gentler girl do the deed.

Looking back, it was cruel, but funny...

This was one of the very few times that I was in 'Helen' mode;

I did have a couple of other clients who were like friends who I could genuinely have a really good laugh with, but I'm glad I didn't do what a lot of working girls do and get on a personal level with them; I've known so many girls to get hurt physically or mentally, or through bribes because the girls refused to not see other men.

Life in Dublin was good, and I was working from a nice apartment with a friend, and generally quite happy. Lots of work coming in. So yes, I was making good money, and never short of men.

One day a client booked in with me for later that same day. My friend let him in, and when he came on through, he looked familiar. I thought maybe he was famous, but I didn't think about it too much, as he could have been a guy I'd seen before and just forgotten. Instead I carried on as normal.

I asked him to take a shower first, like I do with every client, and we were having the usual chit chat, which included him telling me he was in Dublin for work, although I'd already worked out from his English accent that he wasn't local.

I always look out for a wedding ring when men arrive, and he wasn't wearing one.

He wanted me to give him a blow job, while also holding a sex toy on his arse. I never understood the appeal of oral sex for a client, as I insisted they wore a condom, so it always made me think it was like asking someone to suck your toe with your socks on.

When it was over I asked him what he was up to for the remainder of the day, which was work, and as he left he recommended a restaurant to me, which I still use to this day when I'm in the city.

After he left, my friend told me she had recognised him, and named a film he was in, so we were able to figure out who he was. But again, as far as I was concerned he was just a client, and it was no one's business but mine and his what happened that day.

CHAPTER SEVEN

I was doing well in Ireland, and built up my clientele over a year. Everyone knows each other in the industry, and I had lots of work coming in.

There was a verified website I used that was where everyone went, and it was classed as the escorting paradise! Even when I wasn't actually doing the job myself, I had a little basher phone, and I'd take calls from clients asking me for a girl, or girls, and I had to pretend to be the girl who'd be doing the job, as clients would never want to speak to a third party.

So yes, I was making good money, and was never short of men for work.

But when it came to men in my own personal life, it was a different matter. I was basically like the Ice Queen, as I never dated anybody while escorting. I rarely had sex actually, either, unless of course it was a client, as to be honest, I didn't want to. When sex is put in front of you day after day, like in the escorting industry, it does put you off; unless it's someone I proper fancied I wasn't bothered. I'd rather sit in my garden and just have a brew!

But then I met this guy…

Laurie used to go to my school, but lived in London at this point, and we started dating. He was the first guy I'd actually properly fancied in a long time, and was sexually attracted to.

In the beginning, I didn't care what he was up to when we weren't together. I was still working in the first couple of months of seeing him (although I told him I was working in a call centre for the NHS!) so I wasn't going to jinx myself by prying into his affairs. He could do what he wanted when I wasn't around, as far as I was concerned.

He had three or four surnames that he used, so I knew there was something not quite right, but I didn't ask, and just kind of ignored it. I knew from the start that he wasn't exactly marriage material, but we had a right laugh, the sex was good, we got on well, and I got away from Bolton a few days of the month to see him.

After about eight or nine weeks, me and Laurie had gone on a date to a theme park. It had been a proper good day, and afterwards I did tell him the truth – that I was an escort. Little did I know that those theme park rides I had been on earlier were nothing like the roller coaster I was about to live out with Laurie...

We had 'the chat' and agreed to become an official couple; we wanted to make a real go of things, so that's when I made the decision that I shouldn't escort any more.

I stopped going over to Dublin, and got a normal job working in admin. Don't get me wrong, it was proper boring, but I had a new guy now and I was trying to be 'normal'; I've never been 'normal' so I don't really know why I thought that would work, anything that was 'normal' never lasted for very long.

One day soon after, I came home from work and he'd moved all of his stuff into my house. I was seething, bearing in mind, I'd been single for six or seven years at this point and was used to my own company, and within a couple of months of being in a relationship he had moved all his shit in, without actually talking it through with me. He wasn't contributing a penny but thought he would fully move into my house. Alarm bells started going off very quietly...

They started getting a bit louder when I met his family. They had a proper weird set-up, his family were so close, but there's being 'close' and then there's being 'fucked-up close'; I know I don't come from the Little House on the Prairie set-up, but my friends are all family-orientated, and they've never behaved in this manner around their relatives.

The first time I met any of his family, we met his sister and her boyfriend in a Hilton hotel by the Thames. I went to hug her to say hello; she totally ignored me and her eyes were all watery; she shouted at Laurie: "Why are you fucking late?" Awks.

It was clear from that moment that new girls were not welcome into the family; I always thought, was it because of something she'd heard about me, or did she not like me from school, but it soon became apparent that unless you were blood-related, you were always second best.

We sat drinking in the bar and at one point I popped to the toilet, but when I came back Laurie had his sister sat on his knee. She was playing with the curls in his fringe. I had no idea what was going on – a twenty-something-year-old guy with his sister sat on his knee, playing with his hair, twisting it around her finger. I went straight back to the toilet to call a friend, as I'd had my fair share of alcohol at this point, so I didn't know if I was being just paranoid.

She was laughing her head off: "Oh My God, get out of there. Just sneak out and go to another bar. I bet you'll meet someone else!"

The thought crossed my mind, but my stuff was all in his room, so mission aborted. Instead I put up with this strange awkward scenario, but the weird shit continued when he turned around to me on a night out and said, "Imagine Helga (what he called me), you in a wedding dress, you'd look stunning, but then again, my sister would be the bridesmaid, and she might out-do you."

"What?" I stared at him. "Why would I be in competition against your sister on our wedding day?" I asked.

"She's beautiful, my sis, so beautiful."

"Well, who would you want to fuck on your wedding night, me or her?"

Michelle was right, I should have left by this point, but I'll admit he had a really nice penis, and that kept me hanging around for a while. Most girls would agree, when the sex is good enough it can be pretty hard to break off; his personality was pure shit, but the sex was so good.

But the relationship was toxic, pretty much from the start. I was addicted to the bad stuff, as was he. I'm no shrinking violet and quite often I knew how to wind him up, and vice versa. When things were good, they were really good, but the bad side outweighed the good. But that still didn't stop me from being a mug – still not entirely sure if I loved this guy or whether I just got in a rut, addicted to the sex and the attention: I don't believe now that I've been away from that shite for so long that I could honestly be in love with someone so disloyal and bad for me, but I've not exactly got other boyfriends to compare it to.

Our relationship quickly went from one extreme of being together, laughing non-stop, pissing around and all of that, to being proper volatile. We would actually get along quite well but as soon as he had any form of alcohol down his throat or any form of drugs up his nostril, then he was an absolute grade-A cunt!

The two things that were winding me up the most were (a) the fact I was sure he was cheating on me, and (b) that the responsibility of paying for everything kept falling on me. I resented the fact that Laurie paid nothing towards the house. He told me he bought and sold cars for a living, which was kind of true, and he also told me he was doing 'stuff' online, whatever that meant, I never really knew what that 'stuff' was, though he took his laptop everywhere he went, and he kept up his old apartment, but we never went there. I always had a hunch that whatever he did was illegal, but I'd never seen anything.

Either way, the subject of how he paid jack shit towards anything was a regular convo.

One night I was sat in a friend's apartment with her and her boyfriend, when Laurie's ex-girlfriend started texting me saying he'd spent the other day with her and that I was making a mug of myself. This girl was a lot younger than me and came from a very rich toff London family that I'm guessing wasn't very streetwise; Laurie preyed on her because her dad was high up in the banking world.

I asked her to send me her number so that this could be resolved once and for all, as I'd heard so many rumours. Laurie had nipped out so I decided to ring her; I wanted to catch him out, if what she was saying was true, I told her he'd be back in half an hour and she should ring me back then, and let's see his reaction.

Laurie came back and my friend was grinning away to herself: she'd already made it pretty clear she thought he was a low-life. Her boyfriend was shitting himself as he didn't know which way this plan was going to go. Anyway, Georgia rang me back and I answered "Hey, are you alright?", being all friendly. Laurie asked me who it was and I said to her "Do you want me to put him on the phone?" He was like, "Who's that?" and I just said it was a friend that wanted to have a word with him.

I passed over the phone and, Oh My God, he threw it straight at the wall, he knew exactly who it was instantly. He got up and started shouting in my face, "You weird twisted bitch" (sorry I never got the chance to say goodbye, Georgia, my phone was smashed!).

He was so furious, I found the whole thing pretty funny,

and couldn't stop laughing even though it was making it worse for him, but I didn't give a shit; at home this would have turned violent, but he would have never dared lay a finger on me in front of my friend.

He got off the sofa while I was still laughing and he left and locked himself in his apartment upstairs. I wasn't having him just walk off – I was now sure what his ex-girlfriend had just told me was true.

I wanted to remain calm and find the spine and balls to leave this twonk; instead, like any woman scorned, I saw red; my friend gave me a champagne bottle and I grabbed a glass coaster; she said, "Go and smash his car up." I smashed every window of his car and I carefully engraved 'CUNT' on every single panel of it as passionately as any Egyptian spent carving his hieroglyphics.

My friend, meanwhile, was cheering me on from the window of her apartment. When I got back up, Laurie came knocking at the door. He stood there asking me to go back with him to talk things through. He swore to God he hadn't shagged his ex, he just said she owed him money and that she hated him being with me; deep down I knew this was shite: what guy in his right mind goes and sees his ex-bird and doesn't slip her one, but because I'd done stuff he didn't know about I just thought it would make everything even.

At one point he looked out the window and saw his car smashed up. Naturally he was mad about the windows, and said: "Have you done anything else, before I find it?" I thought about the words scratched in the side. Erm... my stomach did about 456 somersaults.

Our relationship struggled on, but I was soon seeing red again. Laurie still didn't pay any money and he was just pissing about, living rent-free at my place; as I'm typing this, my toes are curling that I never had it out with him directly, but just did shit behind his back all the time. I thought it was easier than having a slanging match. It doesn't even matter if the person realises. The satisfaction I get from knowing is enough. At the beginning we both knew we were both up to stuff (great foundation, I know) but when I'd put the seedy life to bed, I wasn't too pleased that his secretive ways were clearly still going on.

Mess with me, and I can do some pretty grim stuff to you!

I used to scrub my feet with this Ped egg and put the dead skin from my feet into the Parmesan cheese and then put it on his spaghetti bolognaise. I did all sorts of other shit too, such as brushing his toothbrush against the dick of a dog on heat. I'd seek revenge in other ways. I know I didn't have the balls to leave him for whatever pathetic I reason that may be, so pulling pranks on him gave me some sadistic satisfaction. With the dog dick, it was prior to him being snipped, so he brushed his teeth with puppies a few times, I wasn't kissing him for a few days anyway.

I'm always up for my friends feeling the benefit of this form of revenge too, and will encourage them when I can! One night me and my friend were drunk and I was consoling her after finding out her boyfriend had shagged an eighteen-year-old in her bed.

I knew she wouldn't leave him, but I wanted her to feel better, so we did the dog and toothbrush trick again while her dog was on heat, then we mixed some of the dog's litter from its tray in with the Kellogg's Crunchy Nut clusters. We pissed in the milk and put a piece of chocolate in my arse crack and put it back in the packet for him to eat.

It didn't half put a smile back on her face…

Another of my friends made a ham sandwich for her cheating

fella with some added ingredients as recommended by me... There's one good thing about men not knowing how to aim in the toilet, as we wiped the bread around it, and I told her to pull snot outta her nose and put it on the cheese. Then we wrapped it up in foil, like a little parcel of purity, and off he trotted to eat it at work, none the wiser.

I was the one my girlfriends came to when they found out their boyfriends were dogging on them, I would come up with ideas on how to seek secret revenge. (If you are in this situation, and you'd like further tips on how to get even, not mad, feel free to email me!)

Despite it all, me and Laurie were still together. But I was skint, he wasn't helping, and I was resenting that I'd given up the money from the escorting for this half-arsed relationship.

I decided I wanted to get away for a few days on my own and make some better money.

The girls I'd been working with in Ireland frequently said if I ever wanted to do their phones there was money there for me. Laurie hated the idea, but I said I needed to go out to Ireland for the weekend to sort them out. I got to the apartment in Ireland and started answering the phones and organising shit; I answered the phone that day to Mr Big, as he was known to the girls; he paid a lot of money and rated the girls highly.

The punternet is a big thing. When I was working the phones in Dublin a guy came over, pure pompous prick, I offered him a drink whilst he waited for his girl, I then introduced them and he went on to tell us how he was a top reviewer, had been to various well-known brothels over the years and was a respected customer. I started sniggering, which confused him. I left the room so I wouldn't come across as rude, but then when I came back in he was on his high horse about his shitty reviewing system.

I interrupted; my friend was quite timid, small in height, sweetly spoken and I feel he was trying to intimidate her. "That's great that you're a well-respected customer. So long as you respect the girls, how many reviews you've left people makes no odds really."

I think he'd quite happily have thrown me out the window, he despised everything about me. He just glared at me whilst this awkward few seconds took place, then walked into the kitchen, and they both left.

But a lot of the girls were really focused on getting five-star reviews, especially off a guy like this one. Ratings and reviews had become a big thing. There was a website where the punters could rate the girls, talk about them, advise on who should go where, etc. It creeped me out a bit, but if they're big reviewers, a lot of the girls will take these guys really seriously. For me, inside my head I'd be thinking "You're no different than any other man who walks in here, you have a dick, you have money, and you're in need of some kind of service."

Another occasion, another ponce who fancied himself as the brass connoisseur, over the phone he told me he wanted a two-girl appointment this day but I only had one girl free, I was just there to make tea and coffee and entertain punters who were there waiting their turn. I put him on hold, when one of my girls was like "Babe, Helen, please do it with me because there's nobody else. It's good money, come on, it's just a one-off, no one will find out, I need the cash, and if he doesn't get his two-girl I'm out of pocket and we'll get a shit review."

This wasn't the initial plan, but I was after the money too, and I felt resentful to Laurie, and in that moment, didn't care.

While we were waiting for Mr Big, I called Laurie and was just chatting casually, telling him everything was going really well with my admin bits and the telephones and that I'd be home very soon. Then I hung up. Or I thought I had. Turns out I didn't! I know people think this only happens in films, but then Mr Big called the other phone to confirm the booking time for one-thirty p.m.

My own phone rang; it was Laurie calling me back straightaway, and he asked what I was doing that afternoon; I just had to lie, so I told him I was going to go shopping because one of the girls had an appointment in the apartment for two hours. He just said, "Okay babe" and we said we'd speak soon, and that's how it was left. I didn't think anything of it at the time and I can't believe I didn't clock his suspicions earlier. At half past one Mr Big came to the apartment and I went into the room with him; it was about forty-seven minutes past one, and it's so weird how I remember it exactly, because most of the time I can't remember what I did yesterday; I could hear my phone ringing nonstop outside of the room, I just had to say to Mr Big that I needed to go and check on it because I thought there might be a problem at home – no one would call me that much unless it was an emergency.

I answered the phone and Laurie was on the other end. "Are you having a nice time, you slut?" I was like "What?" He put the phone down on me and I called him back and went ballistic at him, I was like, what the fuck is your problem? How could he know where I was, don't just ring me up and start slagging me off, and then put the phone down.

I immediately lost my shit: I started smashing up the apartment. Mr Big came out of the bedroom and I told him to get away from me, he was the last person I wanted to see right then; the other girl on the job with me was shouting at me: "What are you doing, Helen?" She was really paranoid about her reviews and didn't want this to ruin them; it's amazing how much call girls take the reviews seriously. She started having a go at me and I told her to get away from me because deep down I knew I shouldn't have taken that job. I was really angry at her, but myself mainly for lying. I hate liars, and I was furious at myself for getting sucked in.

I ran straight outta the apartment and Laurie rang again. I answered the phone as cool as a cucumber.

"Where are you?" he said.

"What are you on about, Laurie? I'm shopping, why are you shouting at me?"

I asked him if he wanted to explain his weirdness and told him I'd called him back but he missed it, and I wasn't going to chase after him.

"Well, tell me where the fuck you've just been?"

I just said I'd been in Pennies, which is the equivalent of Primark in Ireland. I was shaking like a leaf by this point but I kept calm on the phone.

"What you bought then?"

"Oh, just a bikini, some knickers and stuff."

Why did I make the situation even worse: can you tell I'd make a shit compulsive liar?

Listing off a bunch of items had trebled the problem.

"Right then, send me a picture of the receipt."

I knew me saying I'd just thrown the receipt away wouldn't cut it.

I ran down the road and straight into Pennies, flew over

to this poor woman and asked her if she'd give me her receipt. She was obviously confused as to why this nutty spangled British bird was asking this, but I begged her and she handed it over.

I swear to God someone was looking out for me that day, because I was incredibly lucky. If he'd had a brain he'd have thought on his feet and said take a picture of where you are now.

This receipt had the word "floral" printed on it and then something to do with briefs written on it. Within seven minutes of that conversation with Laurie, I sent him the picture of this receipt and it worked out that I'd bought the stuff on the receipt four minutes before the conversation.

It was perfect timing and a perfect receipt.

He said: "I don't know how the fuck you've just done that, Helen, but you better get your arse on the next flight home."

I said, still playing things calmly: "Why do I have to come home?" But really I was taking the piss, considering I was the one that had been lying. He told me to get my arse home and said he wasn't comfortable about where I was and who I was with, then he put the phone down.

I took the phone from my ear and was physically sick in the street. I had really screwed up and I felt guilty for it, God knows why as he was probably doing all sorts, but I just felt so shit and annoyed at myself. Then again, how could I seriously raise a household on my own with just my little amount of money coming in? I could've made so much more money if I had wanted to, but the mess I had made of it after lying just once meant it was good that I stopped it there, if only for my own sanity.

I felt so sick at what I'd done, and exhausted by all the lying and the cheating; however, he was so calm that I had to question in my own mind whether he had gone off and cheated himself that day, as revenge. It was like there was some mutual vibe that we both knew each other had done something that day.

In a way, I lost some respect for him – maybe this is how people feel when they go on to continually cheat on their partners. It's like when you've done the dirty you lose a bit of respect for the person who accepts it.

Not that he had really accepted it – whenever he had a drink he would bring up Ireland again at any opportunity, and say that he knew something had happened. One time he threw money at me, while making accusations about that day.

"Now he gives me money!" I thought. Ironic, as there was still no input from him in that department. He was living in my house rent-free, eating and drinking everything I bought, and not contributing a penny. I often ended up paying my landlord late, or in instalments, as I couldn't afford it, but every time it was me struggling to deal with it on my own. The simmering resentment was still there, but I didn't really know how to change things.

When I relay it all back, I want to punch myself in the face because it was so toxic. But the one positive I can say about Laurie was that he was as good as gold around my boy, very caring, responsible on some level, so I could never knock him for that, but as soon as my son wasn't there things could explode at any time…

CHAPTER EIGHT

I was lying in bed one morning while Laurie had gone to do the school run. He usually went out all day afterwards, but this time he rang and asked, "Where are you now?" and I just said lying in bed where he'd left me.

"Don't get out of bed, I'm coming back."

He came straight back and laid in bed with me, we started shagging then he asked me again: "Helen, what happened that day in Dublin? I want to know."

Then ... BOOM!!! No, I didn't come ... but somebody else did...

Someone had booted my front door off.

The next thing I know, the police are in my room and we're both getting arrested. I had no idea what was going on.

"Erm, what the fuck is happening Laurie, please can someone tell me?"

I was still naked but they let me get dressed, and all Laurie could say was, "Helen, don't say anything to them", and "Keep your mouth quiet". They were dragging him down the stairs while I was shouting: "What have you done?"

"Don't say a thing, babe."

I was panicking as I didn't know what I was about to need to lie about. He'd given me no indication of what was happening. I was so grateful that my son was at school, thank God he missed all of it.

"Why am I being arrested?" I asked again. The police said it was on suspicion of supplying firearms and I was just like "What the fuck?" I didn't even know what the term meant, "supplying firearms".

I told them I didn't have a clue what they were talking about but they took me away to the police station, they just left me sat there in a cell for what felt like forever.

I was shipped around different stations for what felt like forever, being brought into rooms to do pointless, endless interviews.

They asked me loads of questions I couldn't answer, and also kept asking me how I bought my bags and clothes. It was really humiliating, but the funny thing was, Laurie didn't buy me anything, so I was more annoyed that he had clearly been making money in some way, and not giving me any of it!

Eventually, after three days I was released, with no charges brought against me. I got back to my house that Sunday afternoon and it was absolutely trashed, the police had well and truly searched it, and it was a bigger mess than my life.

Meantime I learnt that Laurie had been keeping guns in my loft and ordering gun parts with my bank cards. He never used to own cards as he thought you'd always end up being cloned, but he was happy to use other people's. More fool me that I hadn't noticed, and how frustrating that all that time he'd been making Christ knows how much money off selling these firearms and he never paid me a penny of it. Luckily the police accepted I had no part in it, but it was a different story for Laurie, who was jailed for several years.

It was now 2009 and it should have been time for me to move on with my life and start afresh. All my friends were telling me he was gone, and it was time for me to find myself again. But I still loved him – I know I sound like someone off Jeremy Kyle – so I went to see him in prison. His mum was ill, and he was stuck inside, and I just felt sorry for him. I didn't have the power to just turn my back.

I had his sixteen-year-old sister move in with me at the time. My friends thought I was totally crazy, supporting this guy in prison and spending my own money looking after his family. But I didn't feel like I could do anything else – his sister needed me. I looked after this girl for approximately three years, kitted her out at university, gave her clothes, and bought her food. I'm not sure it was exactly appreciated, but I don't regret it. What else could I have done?

I was doing some serious juggling in my life. On top of the fact Laurie's mum was on her deathbed, I was trying to work, look after his sister, visit Laurie in prison, and bring up my own son.

The one thing I was glad of was that everything around Wayne seemed to have died down. It was now over a year since I'd slept with him, and Jenny was pretty much out of my life, although I would put on a friendly face if I ever saw her, to keep her sweet. But this is my life which, as you know by now, means you can never rely on even just that one thing going smoothly.

Because, what do you know... Bang! Bang! Bang!

Yep, you've guessed it. Not the police again, but that low point of my life, which I mentioned at the start of the book, was just about to begin.

The press were at my door about Wayne Rooney.

They didn't knock once or twice though, they kept on knocking, each time seeming to have a bit more information.

"We know who you are and what you've done, Helen."

"You don't know anything, you twats!" I'd scream, and slam the door in their faces.

I couldn't believe so long had passed with nothing being mentioned, and now suddenly, here it was, ripping right through the centre of my life. I'd forgotten about the blip that was Wayne by then: it meant nothing to me, it was a job, for God's sake.

A few days later I got a notification off one of Jenny's friends saying Jenny had gone into hiding and the press knew absolutely everything; I was like, "Get me on the phone to her now!" I wanted to know what was going on.

Looking back, I fell right into her trap, but I really wasn't thinking straight. She spoke to me for about thirty seconds, and I'm sure she was with the press at that time and most likely had me on loudspeaker.

"I've got no idea," she said. "I can't talk for long. But I haven't told them anything about you."

Yeah, right. Now I understand how the press works, I'm ninety per cent sure there was a Dictaphone recording, as I told Jenny she'd better not have mentioned anything about me and she should keep it between her and Wayne.

Turns out Jenny was showing the press all my texts and messages on Facebook to the journos, which was me basically admitting it. After being waved an extra £10k on top of the 80 she'd already made, she dropped my name like a sack of shit and brought up a pic of my face on Facebook for them to see.

I couldn't deal with that shit now, as I had just too much going on in my life.

I've found out since that loads of texts to so-called friends were being forwarded on to journalists at £250 a pop. I'm in no way blaming anyone for what I did, but how people who had sat with me on nights out, acted as my friend, and who I had confided in, could then cash in by screenshotting evidence of my distress, I'll never know. Those who chose a pittance of a payment and betrayal, over keeping quiet, are two-faced little worms and over the years since I've taken great pleasure in telling them that to their face.

With the help of Jenny and these 'friends' the interest only seemed to get bigger. The next day there were load of press outside my house. I hadn't been named in the papers at this point but she had – her story was all over the News of the World and she was even on the front page. My phone rang and it was my mate Mark. "Oi, have you seen Jenny in the paper? Who's the other bird?"

Cue the world's most awkward arse-twitching pause.

"Heleeeeen, it's you, innit?!"

A lad being a lad, naturally he's in fits of laughter, which to be honest I needed. As things became more serious, my lad friends around me making light of it, laughing and taking the piss out of me, was what I needed.

After my nervous laughter stopped, he had another question.

"Hang on, so were you a brass too?!"

That's when it hit me like 578 sacks of shit, that absolutely every human I knew would know this within the next few days. Soon I would be known as Home Wrecking Whore No. 2.

What a time to be alive, eh?

We started talking more seriously then, and as Mark bluntly put it: "Everyone is gonna know, so sell your story and get what you can."

I just didn't want anything to do with it, I didn't want anyone to know I was involved either.

He was right, and I could kick myself even now for not listening to his advice, and that of a couple of other friends. I lost a lot of money because I was too busy being a soft-arse and thinking I'd wake up the next day and it would all have blown over. I really wish I'd cashed in from day one, but I wasn't as media-savvy then as I am now. For the record, the phrase 'Today's news is tomorrow's chippie paper' isn't always the case, but at the time that's what so many people close to me kept saying. What else could they say, I guess?

Michelle came over after I dropped my son at school. I had all the curtains shut at my house as the press were hanging outside, so I was sat in the dark in the front room, curled up like a lunatic, refreshing the news on my laptop. As soon as a story appeared I read the first few lines and within seconds I'd seen bullshit, and didn't feel ready to face the full article. The odd glimpse of sheer lies is enough to send anyone over the edge.

Bless Michelle, she was trying to help and could see what a mess I was in, but she was heavily pregnant by then, and I was worried about getting her involved. I didn't know where else to turn though, so when she told me to gather my stuff and stay at hers, it seemed like the best choice. But we couldn't even get through my front door without being swamped, so we had to make a plan. Michelle opened the door and shouted to all the press that she needed to get out of the house and told them to move away, as she thought they wouldn't mess with a heavily pregnant lady.

Meantime I climbed over the back fence.

"Helen isn't here," she told them, and locked up the house, then drove round the back for me. I just remember getting to hers and she said, "Helen, you know this is happening, right?" But I couldn't cope with what was going on.

Meanwhile I had clueless Laurie calling me from prison demanding postal orders from me.

Then he added: "Have you seen the papers about that Jenny bird? They're saying another bird was involved ?" He kept naming different girls. I was silent and couldn't talk, and he then said, "Fuck, it's you, isn't it? It is, isn't it, Helen?"

I said yeah, but it was over a year ago and nothing to do with him. We weren't even together when it happened. He went ballistic. "Of all the places I am, I'm in here; everyone's gonna find out. They're listening now, coz all phone calls are recorded."

Michelle told me to get off the phone to him, pointing out that he was the least of my worries at that time. She added that I couldn't hide away forever and I needed to deal with it, and she constantly asked me what I wanted to do. The press by this point had found out where she lived, and had all moved themselves to outside hers.

I didn't want to put any more stress on her when she was so close to giving birth, so I decided to call Rob, a good friend who was that chilled he was almost comatose. I knew he was a good person to have around at the time. He just laughed when I called and was like, "What have you been doing? Tell our Rob what's going on."

"Well, my life is a mess, where do I start?"

And I told him everything.

He was the perfect person to speak to, and thank God he had contacts in the media and football world.

I was able to get in touch with Paul Stretford, Wayne Rooney's agent, and he agreed to see me.

I went to his office in Manchester, and it was horrendous when I first walked in, as he looked me up and down, and it was clear he thought I was this kiss-and-tell girl who wanted to get money and blackmail them, when that wasn't true.

I said to him "You can stop looking at me like that, I'm not here for the reasons you think I am, all I'm arsed about is keeping my name out of it and out of the newspapers."

This conversation was all recorded, possibly even filmed,

I wish to God I could have played it to all the morons who to this day said I set out to ruin Wayne Rooney's marriage. As I'm repeatedly saying, I didn't want anyone to know I was a prostitute, Wayne was like any other client to me, I wanted to keep myself anonymous and out of all this circus bullshit.

Legal action was being taken to try and stop the stories, and I said I'd lie and say Jenny was a liar and nothing went on. I told him I'd say we went to the hotel and nothing happened, that Wayne bailed last minute and couldn't go through with it, and after that Jenny chose to blackmail him and taunt his life. I told Stretford to liaise with Wayne and do whatever he needed to do, and I think he believed I was serious, and knew I just wanted cover. I couldn't afford an injunction of my own, or to go up against the press, but it was something Wayne could easily afford to do.

Anyone who knows Jenny and has seen her on TV can see that horrible, devious side to her, if we'd got the chance to both go to court the judge would have believed my story over hers: sadly we never got that far. I say sadly, but things have turned out amazing for me, maybe not for her.

A friend who knew Wayne advised me I just needed to lie about what time it happened as Coleen believed it happened at night and we were just pissed-up and had gone back to the room. I was like, okay, just someone tell me what to say and I'll say it, all that matters is I don't want anyone to know I even slept with him.

I hold my hands up, I was happy to lie to Coleen and everyone! I just wanted to save my arse.

But then Wayne's people asked me to sign something so I rang Mark, who's in his late fifties, and a solicitor, and thank God I did: he said Helen, don't sign a thing. He said if it goes to court and Wayne gets the book thrown at him, which he probably will because he's done this before, they'll then toss you to the wolves and you'll ruin your chance of making any money for yourself, but everyone will still know you were a prostitute.

So I told Wayne's people they'd have to take my verbal word for it, but I begged them and said I had a son, over and over again. I didn't want any money, I just didn't want my name coming out.

"Just protect me and I'll say what you want me to say."

I didn't want the nation to know I was a brass. I needed to protect my son. Despite what people think, he'd never seen this other side to me.

It went to court and I got the dreaded phone call saying the court weren't having any of it, as Mark had predicted they threw the book at Wayne and it had be confirmed and my name was free to go in the paper the next day.

I went back to Rob's, I couldn't speak, I was falling apart. I told him I didn't want to know anything but when he drove me over to Michelle's the next morning to pick some stuff up she said "Helen, have you seen the newspapers?" Lee had gone to the shop that morning and picked up a newspaper, it was on the bed behind her, but I couldn't look at it.

I spent five days cooped up in Rob's spare room, and didn't eat, sleep or speak. I wanted to run away and hide from the world. The time for my friends to make light of this shitty situation was passed. I don't expect people to understand who don't have kids, but to feel like you can't look your child in the eyes, like you're the biggest, most disgusting failure and that they'd be better off without you being there, has to be the worst feeling I've ever had as a mum. It's meant to go the other way – your child to disappoint you and get in trouble. How the hell was I meant to coach, guide, lecture this dependant ever again, when I'd fucked up this badly?

I'd always called people who commit suicide selfish up until this point, could never figure why anyone would think death would be an option for anything, but then I became one of those people, I couldn't see the wood for the trees and the thought of what damage I'd caused to my son was getting too much to bear, I didn't wanna be here anymore.

I didn't want to face the papers, I even thought my phone was bugged, the only saving grace was Laurie, who couldn't get hold of me. I never wanted this, no matter what anyone says I honestly didn't want it to turn out like this.

In amongst all this crap, Michelle went into labour, but I couldn't leave Rob's house because there was press everywhere. They didn't know I was at Rob's, but they were about. Michelle just said, "Don't worry Helen, you'll get to meet the baby soon."

That killed me!

My best friend, and my world; the pregnancy was so special, and I was so excited for her to give birth. Jenny stole that moment from me and I would never get it back. I didn't meet him until he was five or six days old, and I hate Jenny for that. Michelle was there the next day when I had my son. I envisioned seeing her son and giving him the biggest cuddle in that hospital, but instead I had to speak to her over the phone to tell her I love her and I'd see her soon. I was so heartbroken and so sorry I couldn't be there.

I'm glad I didn't look at the papers too soon because if I'd read anything, I don't know what I would have done, I really don't. Finally Rob said to me, "We don't have to look at anything, but we need to talk about it."

I just said I didn't understand why someone could do this to me when I had a child. I was crying, like an absolute mental case:

"Waaaaaah … Why has she fucking done this to me? I can't do this…" I cringe, looking back.

"Helen, you need to not feel sorry for yourself," Rob told me.

But all I did was be a friend to that girl. I begged her to not say a thing about me, she could have still made money, she didn't need to add details. The whole reason it sold the way it did was because it was a threesome.

"I need to be honest with you, Helen," Rob said. "I've been speaking to the press while you've been hiding. I have friends at the Mirror and you're losing money every single day."

"I'm telling you, all I want is for someone to put a bullet in my head!" I snapped back.

"You've been in the paper every single day, Helen, so in a way you're through the worst of it."

I had been on the front page for days, maybe even a week, and I still refused to look at it.

"Listen," said Rob, "It's better to be depressed with money behind you rather than depressed and skint at least you'll be able to go away with the money."

He advised me to go with the Mirror because they were offering good money. He'd been liaising with the Sunday Mirror about me telling my side of the story; Jenny the previous Sunday had sold her bullshit to the News of the World. The Sunday Mirror agreed to come and pick me up, but I wanted to go to London with Rob; they took me into hiding; it was absolutely ridiculous at some points, getting from the hotel lobby to the restaurants. I had to put a table cloth over my head, walking around like some poor excuse for a Halloween costume, hiding from the public – I'm pretty sure they were taking the piss out of me, but they said everyone knew my face by now.

They said, "Before we do anything you need to see what all the newspapers have been writing about you for the last week."

You have to bear in mind, I'd seen nothing! I hadn't been in touch with the human world, I'd been a recluse for a week. They knocked on my room and asked if I was ready to do this. I said, "Yeah, okay, fine."

But I totally was not ready to do this, I wasn't prepared for what I was about to see. They lined every single paper up on this king-size bed with my face all over them, and all I could see were vicious bullshit headlines. Some said that I was on drugs, some said I was a prostitute to fund a drug habit, a prostitute mother, you name it, I was called it, and I just lost my head. I ripped everything up in the room, I went insane, I smashed everything, there were about four journalists, a cameraman, and other people including Rob. I didn't want anything to do with it, I looked at them and thought, what are you going to do to me now? I saw everything, loads of articles in front of me.

Rob was just like "Give me a minute with her." I just sat on the bed crying and I said to Rob, "What the fuck is all this?" He said, "Helen, it's bullshit, and it's your time to tell them it's bullshit."

I still don't trust all press now. I pick and choose carefully who I 'risk' talking to. I realise now that headlines need to sell.

I was advised to take the 'woe is me' route and play the whole 'Mum' card, literally the worst thing I could have ever done, though. They said they were going to do this lovely Mum article showing I never wanted to be a kiss-and-tell girl, and they'd paint me as the innocent party, all I wanted people to know was that I never set out to hurt anyone.

And I didn't! I didn't want to hurt anybody, I didn't even want to hurt Coleen – did I ever want to hurt her? No. She's never done anything to me, the only time I would want to hurt somebody is if they hurt me directly, or my child or my friends.

This is totally not what came out in the story, though. I got the front cover but it was a total nightmare. I wanted to read it on my own, and while I now know the headline is what sells it, this one was "Helen slept with 500 men for £195 an hour".

The way they reached that fantasy line was by asking: "How many men did you sleep with, Helen, when you were escorting?"

"I have no idea," I replied. What do they think people did? Do they think we sit at the end of the bed with a tally chart going, "Oh look, there's another one!" But because of how stupid they were, they laughed and said, "Is it between 50 and 500?" and I said, obvs, yes.

That story did me no favours whatsoever, it was all bullshit, it was my worst nightmare, for Christ's sake, no amount of money was changing how I felt at this point.

Money seriously means nothing when you've lost your dignity, integrity and privacy, so bear that in mind, any lowlife scheming daft bitches reading this thinking that a quick kiss-and-tell and a deal will gain you a fancy life. Don't get me wrong, I'm fine, and I have been for a long time, BUT it took me a while to get to that point. I didn't see what they were doing at the time as they were asking things about my childhood, and then they changed my words and said I'd lived in this amazing neighbourhood and then I turned to prostitution, there was no proper information in between, they totally screwed me over, none of it was my words.

My words at the time wouldn't have been as interesting to some people, but they wanted to make it look like I was an affluent child who woke up one morning, turned down her caviar and dressage lessons to sell her arse – quite the contrary.

The Daily Mail did the exact same thing, they wanted to make it look like I was this ungrateful bitch that had been given a lifetime opportunity to live in a nice area with parents that did respectable jobs, and I just turned out to be some hussy. I never went out the house when I went home, I saw my friends but never left, that thing had ruined me, aka Jenny Thompson with her hairy nipples! She should maybe have spent more time plucking her nipples than trying to fuck people's lives up.

Part of the story came with a video of me publicly apologising to Coleen, and I did get really teary-eyed, but it was more because I'd been shooting all day for eight hours, and I do cry if I'm really hungry and if something bad is going on, so me starving plus stress isn't a very good mix!

I'd also been talking about shit I didn't want to talk about and being known globally as a prostitute and then having to apologise to a woman whose marriage I'd apparently wrecked.

Was Wayne not the one in the wrong here, anyone, hello?

But my apology was actually sincere, I did mean it, I got ripped to shreds off my friends for crying whilst doing it. Which I eventually found funny, but I was so emotionally drained and still not coming to terms with what I'd done to my kid, my life and other people's lives who didn't exactly deserve this level of humiliation.

But I'm guessing me being on TV and doing other interviews only continued to hurt Coleen; that wasn't intentional, but there was no way I wasn't milking it for everything I could.

In my view, at the time my life was in tatters and I preferred the tatters to at least come with money. Some people would say I should have sold the story straightaway, as he's a dog for cheating on his wife. I don't feel like that at all – I was an escort, if it wasn't for the likes of him how would I have ever got paid for doing the job, without men like him the job wouldn't exist; doing that job doesn't mean you can have your cake and eat it, you can't have money off a man with the intention of ruining his life.

When it comes to Coleen, I've said some pretty shit things in interviews about her, when I've felt angry and bitter about Wayne not paying for an injunction. I've made bitchy comments like, "She deserves it, because she doesn't leave him." Now I'm older, I realise the woman needs to be left alone, and I regret anything I've said along the lines of "It's her own fault."

Some women put up with cheats, but it doesn't mean good people deserve to be hurt and humiliated. She's a mum, raising her kids with a man who she loves. What she puts up with is none of mine or anyone else's business. Everyone has got shit going on, it just so happens that some people's problems seem to be more interesting than others.

I was a lot more hard-faced then than I am now.

When I was out in a bar in Manchester about a year ago both Coleen and Wayne walked into the bar; most of my friends were completely chilled about the situation, but one friend started flapping: "Do you think we should leave? I don't want it to kick off, do you think we should go?" I put it bluntly: we're not going anywhere, we've spent all afternoon in here, we've just as much right to be here as them. Naturally I did think, would it be best for me to leave, and I would have done if I'd slept with him and purposely stitched him up, but that wasn't the case, so I'd done nothing wrong. I avoided them, but on the way out we went to the toilet; he was looking down at a menu, and he clocked me walking past straightaway.

I left immediately after that and have never seen him since. I've never heard from him either, apart from a tweet that came out that he 'liked' saying "I would like Helen Wood under a Christmas tree", but apparently he got hacked; funny how this hacker didn't put anything else; if you got hold of Wayne Rooney's Twitter account you'd do a lot more than 'like' a tweet, mmmmmm.

Many people were still telling me to strike while the iron was hot with press and publicity; I'd locked myself away in my house when Max Clifford got in touch. He told me to go down and see him in London to chat a few things through; I obviously knew who Max was but it took me a bit of convincing to go. In reality I was still hoping the whole thing would just disappear. But I knew it wouldn't, and decided that if I kept my involvement, at least I might have some control over what was written about me.

A girl called Denise, who worked with Max, told me that to make the most money, I would need to do a shoot with Jenny. Not a chance in hell was I going to do anything with that girl. I didn't want to speak to her, go near her, or do anything to make the press associate us even more.

Denise said to me: "If you want to make money from this, you need to put your differences aside."

I was skint. I'd not been paid yet for the newspaper chat, and I'd not been able to go into work. I was also worried about making money down the line – who was going to hire me after all this? So I listened to Denise, and decided I had to suck it up.

We did a shoot with Jeannie Savage, who's a famous glamour photographer. Savage by name savage by nature, so I was a bit scared to work with her, but thankfully she was nice to me, as I just got on with it and did what I was told, while Jenny kept kicking up a fuss about the way she looked. I was embarrassed and felt like an absolute twat posing about in underwear, but that's the only way I could bleed this bollocks situation dry. Jeannie was brutal with Jenny and didn't care for her diva ways, so I kinda enjoyed that shoot, watching the little tramp get put in her place.

Afterwards we were getting food, and Jenny kept denying she'd told the press my name, and said she'd never do that.

I told her it had ruined me, and that I had no money. I kept thinking of all the cash she'd been paid to betray me.

Then she offered to help me out. We went into a bank, and she gave me £1,000 in cash.

It was the most degrading thing ever, taking that money, much worse than taking it off any client I've ever had. "Let me know if you need any more next week," she said, dead casual.

I was happy to have the money, but I wanted to punch her. I'd practically had to beg for her help, and now she was handing me money like I was a charity case. Money that she'd earned through bringing me down.

The staff fobbed her off, they couldn't be arsed with her, so it ended up me having meetings on my own. I confided in Max and he said, "We can protect you in other areas." I told him everything that had happened with Paul Stretford, and I just said I didn't want that to happen again. He said if you tell us anything you know, we can always protect you from it, he said any clients I'd slept with that were famous he could go to court now and get an injunction against them to protect me; he was just acting the big hero, the big I AM. So, I told him some people that I'd slept with, including the actor who'd booked in with me in Dublin. His fame had grown since his visit, so he seemed a relevant person to mention.

I had an interview with the News of The World, talking about escorting, and superinjunctions. Now my take on it was that if

I was allowed to be named in a news article then the guy should be as well. Don't just name the girl, name both parties, it shouldn't matter who's rich and who's not. I had grown quite bitter towards cheating celebs at this point after Wayne kindly didn't foot the bill for my injunction after me agreeing to lie and trying to save his marriage. The woman I met, from the News of The World, was called Carole Malone; she was one of the top journalists there, I was talking to her and we did this story and it was pretty sweet considering it was the News of The World, because they were the biggest paper then. After we'd finished interviewing about who I'd slept with and superinjunctions and all this shit, we found out that the actor had taken an injunction out on me.

Why had he done that? It was all a bit of a coincidence, wasn't it? Max Clifford was just saying he was going to protect me from things like this, but turns out he'd managed to use the information to his advantage. Rather than thinking about me, Max had actually gone behind my back, gone to this man's agent and said, "Helen is going to sell a story on you."

So, quick as could be, off they went to court with the same lawyer that did Paul McCartney's divorce, Charlotte Harris, to apply for a superinjunction to prevent the actor's name being revealed in the press. I'm sure that must have been pretty expensive, and who knows how much Clifford made out of it on the actor's behalf. But the court granted the injunction, and while yet again, somehow it was ok for me to be named in the papers, this guy's identity was withheld from the UK press. The 'UK' bit being key – the ruling didn't apply to the rest of the world. This actor had become well known in the US too, so it received plenty of coverage there.

Once the story was out in America, I told my side of it there – I'd learnt from the Wayne experience that keeping quiet didn't work. Once again, another wife was publicly humiliated, but it's not the wives I feel sorry for – she has a choice in who she is with – but the kids.

If I'd needed confirmation that the actor had been told by Max that I was wanting to sell a story on him, as opposed to me having given him the information to protect it, I got it when I made a TV appearance.

For some reason I'd been scheduled by Max for the BBC1 TV show Newsnight. That's right, the heavy, serious show that focuses on all the important international stories of the day. I'd not watched it before, so didn't have a clue.

Turns out I was on with Hugh Grant, Charlotte Harris, Fraser Nelson, who was editor of the Spectator and some feminist, to debate whether superinjunctions are a good or a bad thing.

I felt like I was in a room with a posse of Stephen Hawkings and dumb-arse me, not a clue what to say. I wasn't prepped for it at all – they may as well have just fed me straight to the lions, because of course I was in the firing line from start to finish.

Thank goodness Fraser, who was sat next to me, was more or less my translator; I'm not down with the legal lingo.

Afterwards, I said to Charlotte, "Why did you attack me like that on national TV? Why am I the one being named and he isn't?"

She replied, "Because you wanted to sell the story."

"But I didn't!" I explained to her that I went to Max and told him who I'd slept with and who might go and get an injunction on me, but I didn't understand why she thought I was selling a story.

"Helen, if I knew any of this we could have protected you," she said.

"Well, it's too late! Why didn't you ring me first, or get in touch with me? You shouldn't have just gone off what some media guru has said to you!"

I felt so stupid, balls deep in a world I didn't know anything about: picture a small fish in a very big pond, that was me. I was sat there like "What am I doing sat in this room?"

I lasted about five minutes, then I snuck home, I wanted to get out of there.

Carole from News of the World, who I still need to thank to this day, rang me after she left the paper and asked to meet in London. "I thought you gave journalism up?" And she said, "I want to meet up off the record and not on tape."

We met near St Paul's Cathedral and we went for a coffee; she said, "Helen, Max Clifford has shafted you so badly, he was behind it all, the whole court case and the actor, and then at the end of it he made himself look like a hero."

Carole went on, "I just don't understand – actually, I do understand Helen, because you're just such a nice girl, you trust and believe people that say they want to help you. If you're going to stay in this world, you need to grow up because you'll get continually fucked over."

And then she said, "I've seen that you've done photoshoots with Jenny, that's fine, to make your money. Just do me one favour when all of this fizzles out? Don't speak to her again."

She said she was the journalist that badgered Jenny for my name, she said she was sat there and waved a ten-grand cheque in front of Jenny's face and she dropped my name quicker than she dropped her knickers for a footballer for free. She said, "I don't know what it is but you get under my skin, and I have a soft spot for you. I thought you were a kiss-and-tell girl, but then I met you and I thought, why is this happening to this girl?" She admitted she shouldn't divulge information like this but she poked and poked at Jenny, and Jenny said it was just her originally. As soon as she offered the extra ten grand Jenny named me in a heartbeat. Carole admitted she could have offered her another fifty grand, but it only took ten.

Jenny went and got a picture out of the two of us, straightaway she found them photo albums and showed them a picture of two girls – me and her on a night out. Jenny also told them where I lived and everything, of course she did.

I pulled away from Max, and the interest in me was starting to fizzle out in London, as it does. One day you're in demand for all sorts of press coverage, and the next day they can't even remember your name, so I headed back home.

It's not a nice thing to admit this but I did really start to get fucked off with men. I grew to be quite cold, kinda like, "Well this is it now, everyone knows what I've done thanks to a man not saving my ass when I was prepared to save his (Wayne)." I began not giving a shit about what people thought, I still don't but not to the degree where it's festering inside and I'm bitter, I became bitter towards men again. Max Clifford was excellent at making me believe I was some form of victim, that men had taken advantage, the irony of this man ever slating another man's wrongdoing towards a woman is almost laughable. Almost.

CHAPTER NINE

I was desperate for a 'normal' life again. Not that my life has ever been normal by most people's definition, but you know what I mean! A bit of peace and quiet, no press coverage, and a chance to spend time with my son and friends.

But first I had to work out what to do for money. There was no way I was going back to brassing. Instead, I wanted my own business.

While all this shit was going on with the press I'd been getting my hair, nails and all my beauty bits done pretty regularly. If I was going to have my face splashed across national papers and TV, I may as well make sure I looked decent!

So I decided I wanted to own a local beauty shop. There was already one up and running with girls working there, so I went and asked about buying it.

Well, this woman, Sharon, saw me coming from a mile off. Me setting up the shop was the equivalent of walking into a hardware store and asking for a rubber hammer and a glass nail, it was the most stupid thing I'd ever done.

I gave this woman £17,000 for the salon, with the idea I'd keep the staff, and everything would keep running as it was. In the back of my mind, I was thinking, why is she selling a good thing? No one ever sells a good thing.

But I was focused on the fact I wanted some self-importance, and to throw myself into something, I wanted something to strive for.

But naive me, I didn't get a contract or sign anything, and 48 hours later I walked into the shop as proud and excited as could be, and not one single person turned up to work for me, no one.

It turns out, Sharon knew all the girls were leaving and that's why she was selling it. Of course I was fuming, but I needed this to work, so I thought it might be better if I had her on my side. We agreed to meet at a local pub to talk everything through, and see what we could work out.

I'd been in this local lots of times before; it was pretty quiet when we got there, and Sharon and I were sat chatting through the business. A little way into the night the pub got busier and a load of girls turned up, including Laurie's brother's fiancée. They were from the other end of Bolton.

Apparently they thought it was funny to all start chanting 'Rooney' really loud and banging on the tables, so obviously now everyone in the pub was looking at me and talking. I said to Sharon that I thought it's time we left, as I just wanted to get outta there. But she persuaded me not to leave because of them. God knows why, when there was nine of them and two of us.

I could see they were drinking and getting more and more rowdy, and a real bad atmosphere was developing. I went to the bar and stood there for ages waiting for our bill. I should have just walked out, to be honest. Next thing I know things had escalated and they were smashing on the tables and hurling abuse at me; Sharon turned around and started gobbing off at them. The girls went fucking mad and one of the nine got up and hit her, so I smacked the girl back.

Probably not the best thing to have done – I should have let them kick the fuck out of her, after all this woman had not only done me over but she provoked a reaction from these strange dickheads that take it upon themselves to try and intimidate girls on their own (well hard). Before I knew it all of them were on top of me, to my knowledge it was two sisters and their dad (a bent cop); three girls beat the shit out of me on the floor, they stamped all over my face, they broke my nose and fractured a rib. The bent copper (who just got out of jail), an absolute knob, filmed this: he didn't help, he just recorded it.

I woke up semi-conscious to him with a phone in my face and laughing at me, he was saying that he'd recorded it all and he said, "Looks like you're going into the paper again." And that's what I woke up to. The people that owned the pub were friends of these girls, one of the bar staff even joined in kicking me in the ribs. I was slumped against the floor when the police arrived, I have no idea who called them because everyone seemed to be in on this beating, my phone and bag had been stolen and I was in a right mess.

The policewoman was hovering above me asking everyone what happened; no one was really speaking except for a young bar lad who was nearly in tears and shocked by what he'd seen. He said everyone just jumped on me and the policewoman said, "Well, why did they do this?" and he said, "Because she slept with a footballer." The policewoman replied, "Well, that's what you get for sleeping with footballers."

I didn't speak, I even zoned out to anything else they were talking about, I asked them to take me straight home.

I always thought when I'm out with my mates I'd want to get revenge on them, but the two occasions that I've seen these dickheads I actually just laughed and smiled, I know so much about their private lives, I got close to one of the girls, Lucy, who told me various stories to do with some of the girls' private lives, sometimes it's just nice to sit back and know you've got the last laugh without having to get physical. For people to behave like this – don't get me wrong, a fight one-on-one is fine, but to intimidate one person yourself, something must have happened to them early in their life. I soon learnt this bent cop had been nothing but a bully to his female family members, no wonder his daughter has turned out scum.

Of course, I was all over the papers again! Sharon had taken photos of me just after I was coming round and sold the pictures of my injuries to the newspapers. In case she hadn't made enough off of me with the salon, looks like she made money off this too.

My nose didn't heal properly, and went funny on one side, so it made a noise when I was breathing. I had surgery to get it reconstructed, but it wasn't about getting a nose job, it was about getting a natural-looking nose, that I could actually breathe through!

People think I've had extensive surgery over the years, which makes me laugh. A lot of it is just good make-up.

The only other things I've had done over the years is my teeth – they looked like Red Rum at one point, so I needed them sorted – and my boobs. They never seemed to be the same again after I had my son, and I'd developed a bit of a complex about them, so getting those done gave me a confidence boost.

I got lip filler for a while, but not anymore, and that is it! People go on like I've had a new head, and choose to believe the most extreme articles and speculation they can find on me, but there you go, that is the Helen Wood surgery truth, straight from the horse's mouth (or not, once I had those teeth fixed…)! Good make-up, filtering and a good set of teeth are everything, and by far my best investment.

Anyway, I tried to put the attack behind me, and get on with running the shop. I threw myself in at the deep end and learnt everything I could, putting in as many hours as possible, to make it a functional business I could be proud of. And for a while, it was.

It was a roller coaster of being ripped off, bailing girls out, and ninety per cent of the time sheer stress, but it taught me that working by myself and for myself is what I'm here to do.

I was still dating Laurie in prison. It wasn't easy, and we actually ended the relationship a couple of times, but I kept wanting to give it the benefit of the doubt. I can slag Laurie off till I'm blue in the face – he was in prison, he'd deserted me – but at times, we got on like a house on fire. And despite the million and one times I could have cheated on him while he was in prison, I didn't once do it. But it really felt like my life was on hold, that I was in this weird limbo, until he came out.

I started visiting him a lot more trying to keep it alive, sometimes I would go to the prison like three times a week, it's kinda strange but looking back visiting Laurie in prison was my escape from stress, as when we got on we really got on. He was moved around to different prisons so I would always be travelling to a new one, it just became part of life. I was in denial constantly though, thinking he didn't want this life and he'd come out a changed man, and things would be all rosy. I sent him money every single week and took care of his sister on the outside, I gave him the benefit of the doubt and thought I'd see what he was like when he came out.

All my friends were changing in their lives, they all had boyfriends, some were settling down, and I just thought: this will do for now. It's actually embarrassing when I look back to when I was young and this relationship, I don't think it was an age thing, I can't really use that as it's such a shit excuse, I think I was needy, I just needed someone to love me, maybe that was it.

When I speak to my clients today, if anyone tells me shit like they're putting up with abusive crap, verbal or physical, or if their partner is cheating, I can't help but say NO! Stop fucking putting yourself through it, please look after yourself girls, make some money, live your life, get on a plane, do stuff, don't waste your life with a man. Girls need to know they're equal and worth so much, and I can't stress that enough to young girls because of the things I went through. I'm not saying don't stick by your man if he's in jail, but analyse them wisely: are they really gonna come out and do the right thing by you? Some do, but most don't.

Eventually Laurie went into an open prison and this is when I thought things might change. I'd set everything up for him at home so it was all perfect for his arrival. I was encouraging him to get back on the straight and narrow, and wanted him to do stuff like the 'normal' world. All along I'd wanted him to come home, as much as he'd been a prick. Looking back I was in cloud cuckoo land, thinking he was going to come home, get a job, and we were going to live happily ever after. I thought we were going to walk the dog at the weekends and make fucking casseroles or travel the world together.

Imagine how horny I was – I was like a nympho in a fucking convent – but I didn't think about it most of the time he was away, I kind of blocked it out of my mind, I wasn't coming home to a guy so I learnt to live without it.

I'd started to think about us being together more, as in open prison he now had day release; I imagined going to pick him up for the first time, getting him in my car and me sitting on top of him and riding him till his dick eroded.

When the day came I drove to the prison and waited outside. I had a raincoat on with nothing but underwear underneath it, suspenders, the lot. I was a bit nervous, but excited.

He came out and got in the car and then for some reason

I did a 180 and everything changed in my head, went completely frigid. Zero sexual emotion going on in my head, almost a two-year drought had come to a head, and the last thing I could think about was getting any of his head. I just didn't want him to touch me, it was really weird, all my sexual emotions drained out of me, I didn't want to be wearing this shit. He tried to kiss me, and wanted me to pull over, but my body froze, I just wanted to drive us home.

When we got home I gave him the whole speech about how he had to do something legal, I said we needed to move on, I didn't want him back in prison and I needed some regular cash coming into the house; he sat me down and we talked about what he could do and he told me how he was going to start buying and selling cars. He also wanted me to take the contraceptive rod out of my arm so we could try for a baby. To keep him sweet I said I would do, I said I'd make an appointment, although thank God I never did.

I'd built so much up around his return, but in the end, it was nothing like I'd hoped. Partly it was me, as he'd been away for so long, I felt like everything was mine; I'd turned into a crank, I'd begun to resent him for all this time he'd been away. He'd empty the dishwasher and I'd bark at him for putting the cups in the wrong cupboard, I'd be like, "They're not your cups," and I'd take them out and put them back in the right place. I fully admit I'd turned into a nagging twat of a bird that couldn't snap out of this resentment I held towards him.

I was also the only one with money, and remembering how I'd paid for everything last time, I made him ask for every penny he needed.

I was angry and resentful, and realised I wasn't over what

he'd done. My best friend also wasn't talking to me, as she was so against the relationship.

I was also in a really good place with my son and I was worried about Laurie rocking it. Me and my boy were spending so much time together, and he was just at this really good stage and becoming my little best friend. While Laurie was still good with him, I felt guilt that I had ever brought him into my son's life.

Laurie has been the only man I've introduced to my son, but as far as I'm concerned that's one too many: it's a learning curve, but a costly one; I brought a bad person into my son's life and I can never change that.

CHAPTER TEN

Things were shit for a while; I still have no idea why I didn't cut him out completely; we eventually did sit down and talk about it all, and he got really upset. He got upset and I listened: I might have been losing it, but I wasn't completely heartless.

Unfortunately he always knew how to pull at the heart strings.

It was then that we decided to book a holiday. He thought we needed to get away and have a break, and so did I, if we had any chance of working this out. I booked Morocco and had to pay for it all of course, but at the end of the day, money comes and goes in my life, and I like to enjoy it, especially with a holiday.

So the morning we were due to go, I was packing at my place, and he was at his house packing his stuff. It was about seven a.m. when he called, and without even hello, said: "Helen, you need to get out of the house now."

I was so confused but he just kept telling me : "Grab a laptop, get out of the house, and come and meet me, I need to talk to you."

It was obvious he was in trouble again. I was devastated, worried and pissed off, all at the same time. I threw the suitcases in the car, and went to the Stockport car park where he wanted to meet. As soon as I saw him I was screaming and crying and letting out all my anger and frustration at what he kept doing to himself, and to me. All very Jeremy Kyle again. He kept saying how sorry he was, but that early that morning the police raided a bunch of houses where he and a friend were growing weed.

At that point I didn't care if he was in trouble for robbing an ice cream, or for murder. It was the fact he was constantly abusing my trust. I would have more respect for this guy if he just told me he was bent, I might have kept on seeing him but wouldn't have let him near my house or my son.

Eventually I told him not to come near me ever again, and headed off to Morocco with my son. I thought the holiday was booked and paid for, I needed to get away, so we went.

But when we got to the hotel, unbelievably, Laurie was already there, waiting in reception with a big smile on his face like we were about to have the holiday of a lifetime. Instead, all I could think of was drowning him in the pool.

I was absolutely drained, and worried that although my son was still so small and oblivious, that while I was his mum, he was seeing part of me as this absolute nutcase, a raving lunatic.

The next day Laurie told me he wouldn't be going back to England, he just said he was going straight to Cyprus, he couldn't come back to the UK and go back to prison. I broke down because I just couldn't understand why he'd done this to me. Why wasn't I enough?

He was only there with us for three days. When he left and went on the run, he travelled through Egypt and who knows where for two weeks, and would ring me off random numbers asking me to send money. Although I knew I was being a mug, I was worrying about him, and would rather have given him money knowing it was keeping him safe.

He eventually got to Cyprus and went to live with his cousin, the one I'd met when we'd been on holiday there, she was always dead nice, so I knew she'd look after him. She seemed like a really level-headed person, the most level-headed in the family.

Things went quieter for a while. Laurie said he was busy and started working at Linekers Bar. It was on the strip, where everyone drinks, parties, fights, and picks up one-night stands.

I imagined what sort of shit Laurie was doing. He would get home at whatever time it was in the morning, and he'd call me and tell me he was in bed, but he obviously hadn't been. My anxiety went through the roof, and some days I just didn't sleep, but lived off coffee and energy tablets. I was also stick-thin.

I've learnt over time to never think that someone has the same morals or heart as you. Just because you're going out with them doesn't mean you think the same or do the same. Even after all this, I would have never looked in another man's direction, but I didn't trust him as far as I could throw him. So after three weeks, I flew out to see him.

I went straight to the bar he was working in, sat down, and he leant over to give me a kiss and instantly I knew everything was different, as the kiss felt so different.

That night the sex felt different too. He didn't look at me or kiss me throughout it, but was just hammering away. It was like we'd just met and this was a one-night stand.

I kept saying to myself I was being paranoid, but I could tell there was someone in that bar that he just didn't want me to see or speak to, by the way he was acting.

Over the next four months I went to visit him seven times, and looking back it was always a disaster. He was taking so many drugs out there that he'd flip and go mental at the slightest thing, and I felt like I always had to be on edge around him.

One day he told me to chill on my own and not come to the strip to see him. He made up an excuse that his work boss would moan at him even if I popped in for a drink, because he wouldn't be working hard because "his bird" would be knocking around. I took a book and headed to the beach for the day, and came back feeling pretty relaxed, so I headed to bed.

I set my alarm for ten p.m. when he was due to finish at the bar, then I woke up and laid out candles everywhere, trying to make the room look nice, and began clock-watching, and looking forward to him coming home from the bar.

Midnight passed, one a.m. passed, it was two a.m. now and he still wasn't back. I went back to bed, knowing that by now he must have got on it, and would be in a right state.

It got to six a.m. in the morning, and I called his cousin. "Has Laurie come back to yours?" I asked, but he hadn't. I went out and started looking for him, like a lunatic, I knew what he was doing and I needed to see it with my own eyes so I'd finally get a grip and leave this prick.

Walking around Pathos crying my eyes out, I just didn't know where he was. I kept thinking maybe something had happened to him, when I'm sure the reality was he was definitely balls deep in some stripper. (I'm even cringing writing this. Wake up Helen, you dickhead!)

I rang his cousin again at nine a.m., still no sign. She told me to come to hers so I wasn't alone, so I headed on over. She made me a brew and calmed me down, but I was just so exhausted from it all. Then in he suddenly wandered. I couldn't even bring myself to look at him, while his cousin defended me: "If you don't want to be with her, just tell her, don't treat your girl like this, have some balls and leave her, or stop fucking about."

I told him not to insult me anymore, because I felt like the biggest mug ever. He was such a mess though, and off his tits, that he wasn't really making any sense. In the end I went out for breakfast with his cousin and left him to sleep it off.

As with every row we had, later that day he managed to turn it on me. He accused me of cheating on him back home, which was one hundred per cent untrue, but was his way of deflecting things. He started hitting me, scragging me around

144

and pulling my hair out, and said, "You show up like you're the perfect bird when you're probably getting shagged by some dickhead at home."

Did that stop me going back over in a couple of weeks though? No. And as always, things were incredibly volatile. I'm embarrassed looking back that I put up with it, but like a typical abuse victim, I just didn't want to let go, or didn't know how to.

Laurie started introducing me to some of his friends, but it felt weird, like they knew the shit he was doing behind my back. He'd changed his job and told me he'd started working in a 'call centre'. I found some relief in this, as I heard him and all his friends talk about business and targets, and although he still asked me to send him cash, he was earning more money. Was he finally on the straight and narrow?

He gave me some cock and bull story about a business he was setting up, he needed £4k to do so, yup, I paid it into his 'business partner's' bank the next day.

I've thought since about why I kept going back. I don't want this to sound like a sob story, or that I'm after pity, I'm not, but I was the loneliest person ever. I would go to work, be a mum and then be a friend to people, but no one saw what I was like in my house at night. The minute that my boy went to bed I would have a glass of red wine, smoke twenty menthols and just cry my eyes out. I never told anyone though. Maybe I should have done, but they probably would have told me to get a grip, I didn't have anything about me anymore and I was losing more of me bit by bit. Things were pretty bleak, I'd lost all sense of who I was and what the hell I was doing. I wasn't sleeping and I had insomnia, so I started going to therapy.

Sitting down and talking to this lady called Deborah Morgan

was so bizarre. I couldn't even talk in the first session because I kept crying. But talking to someone outside of my normal circle, who didn't know them or judge me, really started to work. She laid it on the line for me and provided a much-needed reality check. Deborah taught me to develop more self-respect and expect more for myself. She also taught me to pity this man, instead of hating him – I should feel sorry for his way of life.

So I went out to visit for the seventh and final time.

Ironically, halfway through that trip, we went out and had a really good night, getting pissed, dancing to cheesy music, and talking about anything and everything. Then we came home, had amazing sex, and it felt like the early days, when things had been good. It was the ideal relationship for a few hours, and I lapped it up.

Lying there after though, in a post-shagathon haze, I was slumped, half hanging off the bed, looking at the floor, and staring me in the face were a set of ridiculous fake lashes, that looked like they belonged to Kat Slater. I picked them up and held them out in front of him. He played dumb and tried to claim they were mine. No chance you'd catch me in a pair like that.

He then said that he had people over and they had parties, but I just said: "Right, and they were doing the worm alongside your bed? Or partying actually in your bed, you prick? No, Laurie, you can't bullshit your way out of this one."

But then, as usual, he began turning it on me, calling me paranoid and a psycho, and losing his rag. Suddenly I felt really vulnerable. I was in the middle of nowhere with this unpredictable nutter who I knew was capable of most things, and I had no one around me.

So I calmed him down, and I just told him I believed him.

In my head I wanted to do something psycho, worthy of a woman scorned, such as setting fire to his shit, but instead I took a deep breath and thought I just needed to get through the rest of the break. It was the turning point for me, when I thought I'd really had enough.

The next – and last – night, we went out for dinner, and I started asking him more about his job. It was like I'd given him permission to open up on it all, and he started boasting about it. Turned out it wasn't quite a customer service line for Sky, or whatever I'd imagined. No. Him and three other lads were ringing old people all over the world, getting them to hand over personal details, and effectively conning them out of thousands of pounds.

"So, you're stealing off people like our grandparents? Ripping them off of their life savings?"

"Not our grandparents." He grinned.

"Same bloody thing!"

Turned out they'd even learnt other languages so they could target people in all sorts of countries. Turns out he must have had a brain of sorts, just not used for anything good.

That did not sit right with me one little bit. Listen, I don't have an issue with dodgy people, drug dealers, Del Boys, etc., far from it, but scamming old folk for their money, there's a line somewhere and he'd done the long jump over it. Wow! Proper. Fucking. Scum.

It wasn't long before he was arrested for all of these fuck ups. I went over for a week and was visiting him in jail, taking him food, then sitting in court with him. He knew I wasn't hanging about, he tried to hold my hand in the court room and I couldn't bring myself to even look in his direction, let alone touch him.

So pull a moony and walk out... But I didn't. I smiled

and nodded, and kept all my anger inside, knowing he had ruined himself.

I'm by no ways proud that I stayed with someone (Laurie) that was subsequently making me ill, and extended the damage that's already been done by former controlling moronic men, I hated myself for being such a mug, but like with a lot of things, I choose to learn from it instead. I'd be gone in a second, the first sign of anyone taking the piss out of loyalty or smothering me. I'm no angel, far from it, I can be an arsehole for no reason at all, I know this too, two feisty people in a relationship were never going to work, again something else I've learnt from.

CHAPTER ELEVEN

After everything with Wayne had come out in the papers, someone from Max Clifford's office called me, to say someone had dropped out of Celebrity Big Brother and they wanted me to go on instead.

I didn't really want anything to do with Max, but I thought the money would come in handy, plus I thought I'd only be in the house a few days, get the cash, and then the public would be sure to send me home. But then I got attacked by those girls in the pub. I called to tell Max I'd been battered and warned him that my face looked pretty bad, and within minutes I got a call back saying they didn't need me anymore.

Then, while I was up the wall with Laurie, not knowing wtf I was doing with my life, smiling on the outside, having seven million anxiety attacks on the inside, Michelle thought she'd cheer me up by doing something totally out of the bloody blue – she put me forward for Big Brother, the regular one this time, rather than the celeb one.

I turned up at hers and she said: "Big Brother are doing auditions, I'm gonna apply for you."

I laughed, and didn't take it too seriously, thinking it was an idea that would get talked about for five seconds, then would fizzle out. I've never been a couch potato, and reality TV cringes me out at the best of times, so Big Brother was never really on my to-do list.

But then Michelle added: "Actually I've already applied, pretending to be you, but they need a video."

She uploaded one of me on a night out, no doubt being a loudmouth, and explained she was applying for her best friend, and they should meet me.

A few weeks later I was in London and was well on my way,

as I'd been drinking most of the afternoon with friends. I put on social media that I was in London when a girl messaged me from Big Brother's research team on Instagram, asking if I had time to meet them for a drink while I was visiting. I read it again, thinking, am I reading this right? Argh, why now?!

"I'm pretty pissed tbh," I typed, "but staying in the Mayfair Hotel if you want to meet downstairs in the bar?"

Within an hour I was sat with these two women having cocktails and debates about the ways of the world. It felt like I was just sat with my mates, so it went really well.

The next day I woke up with the world's worst hangover, stuck to my friends, all in the same bed, panicking: "Christ, what was I saying to those two, what if I've said something I shouldn't have?" (Highly likely.) Me + copious amounts of gin = hefty dose of anxiety. I hadn't discovered Xanax back then…

A few days later the phone goes, and it's one of the BB posse asking me to go to an audition in Manchester and they'd see me again there, amongst the other applicants. Yep, sound, I'd be there. It all became a bit of a whirlwind after this (if you didn't think life had been until then!).

The day arrived and surprise surprise, everything that could go wrong, goes wrong. I had my hair and make-up booked in so I'd look good, but two of my girls were off sick in the salon so I had to do five spray tans for customers and didn't have time to get myself ready. I turned up at the audition late, chippie head (greasy hair), barely any make-up on, in my work clothes, more resembling Alice bloody Cooper. I sat there fuming with a face like a melted welly, and a number stuck to my chest.

I looked around the room and thought wtf am I doing here with a bunch of over-eccentric weirdos desperate to get on this show – girls talking to me with strange Malibu accents and tits out in my face. What did they think they were applying for, Big Brother or Babe Station? I was in black leggings, Doc Martins and a black t-shirt with a crow on it. I looked like the Grim Reaper, I mean you're meant to go and stand out – I guess I must have somehow.

While I was still in the waiting room, a lad pranced over and straddled a chair in front of me: "So babe, tell me all about yourself, let's pretend this is your audition. Go!" I paused, took note of how this person was way too involved with my personal space, and said: "Please can you leave me alone, I'm in a bad mood." That sounds rude, but I said it in the nicest way possible... The majority of the room seemed to be annoyingly fake though, and I thought about bailing.

The audition process lasts for two days. People think because I slept with a footballer years before, that I got queue-jumped. Cringe. I wish I could show you the facial expression I pull when plonkers assume that's why I got on the show. Nope, I had to do all the auditions, and when I say they're long, they are LONG.

The debates, though, were amazing, I was right in my element. Shit mood? Don't like anyone else in the room? It's showtiiiiime. There were around thirty of us in the room for a debate on 'Should immigrants be allowed to work in the UK?' Go to one side of the room if you thought Yes, the other for No. Only me and a few other people said Yes. When some smellbag from the other side was going on about "They're taking all of our jobs, that's why there are none left for the English people," I replied: "Actually, you'll find that the jobs a lot of these people do are the jobs the lazy bastard 'English,' as you put it, won't do. It's a cop out for people not wanting to work. It's not about people taking all the jobs."

Naturally I got pissed on as there was a lot more noise from the other side of the room, and I don't like being interrupted. So I soon shut it down with a simple: "Your point is shit, mine is not."

I then had to sit in the corridor with them knowing how much I already wasn't liked, and this was just the audition. Call me a miserable bitch, but I didn't like a single person I was in the room with that day. But I wasn't there to mingle.

Thousands of people had been sent home after the first day, and then jackpot, I got invited to the final interview stage, which was to sit in front of the producers of the show. I was in there with five people, including the twins Sally and Amy, who went on Big Brother two years later (ten out of ten for persistence for them).

We sat around the room and felt like we were being interviewed for murder or something. I was the oddball, that was clear from the start, and it's where I thought I really messed things up. Everyone got on really well – aka licked each other's arses – and I just sat on the end like something out of The Omen.

We had to stand up and say "What is my claim to fame?" and God's honest truth, I was like, what, I don't have a claim to fame! I panicked, as I was clueless as to what I could say.

One of the twins stood up and proudly announced that they had been on a date with Cristiano Ronaldo. A voice in my head replied: "Pfft, well, I've scored a hat trick with that team, so sit on that one." But luckily another voice in my head told it to shut up! I can't actually remember what I did come out with in the end. I'd love to watch the audition back, as it must have been something really shit, or a lie.

Someone told a sob story and because it was a reality show audition, everyone started hugging each other and gushing about it, while I remained sat on my chair muttering "Weirdos."

We'd all been asked to bring an item with us that represented us. I took a stress ball shaped like a cock (what?!) and explained that I had it because I'm a bit of a stress-head.

The girl next to me was my nightmare kind of person – one of those petite girls that uses their height as a way to act cute and thick, which really gets on my tits. She'd brought a cuddly toy along. She put on a five-year-old's voice and said she took it everywhere, and went on to play with the paws of the teddy while talking as if he had a voice. "I brought my bunny wiv me cos he's cute, and I love him, and on the way here he fell out of the car, that's why he's all muddy."

It might sound harsh, the temptation to elbow her in the head was there, but everyone else in the room except me and the producers were going "Aww babe, that's so cute."

Instead I was sat there like Victor Meldrew muttering "Twat" under my breath, and by this point was suffering with my usual facial Tourette's. I find falseness like this unbearable.

I'm still friendly today with one of the producers, and he told me that none of them knew who I was at the audition, and I was taken at face value, which is nice to know. He told me it was the exact moment the girl was banging on about her teddy that they decided they wanted me on the show. Once I'd left the room they zoomed in on my facial expressions and constant muttering while everyone else bum-licked, and that's what bagged my ticket into the house. I knew it would come in handy one day! So I'd like to set the record straight, these producers didn't know me from Adam, nothing at all about Wayne. I got in based on the fact I am naturally a miserable person around fake-arse twats!

When I left the audition, though, I called Michelle and said I'd messed it up, as no one had got to see the fun side of me. She reassured me: "Don't worry, they'll want you because you weren't fake."

A few more meetings later, and I was in the salon, when a lady from Big Brother called. "Can you go somewhere quiet?" she asked.

I legged it upstairs like a little kid.

"We need to ask you a question, Helen. Would you like to go on Big Brother?"

"Waaaah, OMG, fucking hell, shit, really, OMG, Yeeeeees!"

After that, things started happening really quickly. I was told I had just a few weeks, and nobody was to know. I was absolutely buzzing. In fact writing this makes me realise that from that exact phone call, my life has never been the same since. Cheesy, but true.

I also went into panic mode – what do I wear, my hair is shit, I need to go to the gym, how will I wax my 'tache in there, should I laser my pubes so no one sees me shave them on camera, where will I go for a shit, what about when I'm on the blob (I'm moody as fuck and cry over everything, that's why that worried me).

All these thoughts were doing my nut in. I was losing sleep thinking about where to take a shit on telly, not really the normal thing keeping a person up at night, and my head started to explode with all these stupid thoughts.

Funnily enough, people have asked me since: "Did you not worry that the housemates will know you've been a prostitute?" etc, but that didn't cross my mind. I was more worried that I would fart in my sleep, as I thought that would be more embarrassing. That sounds back-to-front, I know.

Meantime Laurie had been brought back to the UK and put straight in the tin. I'd found out other information in recent weeks.

Throughout the period of Laurie living in Cyprus he said he didn't want me on any social media. I didn't check immediately, but as you Facebookers know you can request to message someone. It turned out a guy who I'd got pissed with in Cyprus in a group one night had messaged me saying, "Hiya, hope you don't mind me messaging you, just wanted to say you're a really cool girl and I think you deserve better from Laurie. I might regret sending you this message but he's living another life out here."

I also received a message after this from a girl explaining how me and her had been passing like ships in the night; the minute he would drop me off at the airport she'd be moving back in. She was living in Cyprus and she told me everything. When I arrived in Cyprus to visit him, he would move her out, and then I would go and he'd pick her up on the way back from dropping me off at the airport.

She was shagging him for months.

I asked for her number and called her to talk about it; she was crying on the phone, she was a lot younger than me, yes she knew about me, and yes she knew I was his girlfriend, I actually didn't give a fuck though; at this point she had no loyalty towards me and I wasn't mad towards her, I told her what had happened and told her to crack on and have the best summer in Cyprus and stay away from dickheads.

All this had built up and he didn't know any of it, although he knew something was up as I kept giving every excuse not to see him, and he'd started sending visiting orders out to other people.

So I decided I wanted to go and see him, as I figured I wouldn't see him again after Big Brother – and I wanted to see his face when I told him where I was going.

I couldn't bring myself to look at him when I was there,

or even say hi properly. He asked me why I was being so cold. "Not sticking by me, are you. I've finally come back so we can be together eventually, and now you can't be arsed."

Wow, he was making out like it was his choice he'd been arrested and was back in the UK. What was he on? After the years of crap he'd put me through, this was just the latest insult.

"I need to tell you something, I'm going into Big Brother."

At first he didn't believe me, then he got so mad, I thought fire and smoke was about to come out of his ears and nostrils. His face was a proper picture, but for the first time in our deranged relationship, I couldn't have been less arsed about what he thought if I tried.

"Why would you go on there, no one's going to like you," he said. Then he continued to tell me that I'd be ruined by the papers, after one night.

But I wasn't going on there for anyone else, I was going on there for me.

There was no physical contact, no kiss goodbye, I just said I'd send his usual postal order on the Monday. And I did – his final postal order of £200 was to get his goodies stacked up for my grand finale night!

I took all my stuff to Michelle's, and I had the nicest week ever with my son before going into hiding; I knew me and Laurie were done and everything started to feel right, I was happy and I was smiling a lot. We all stayed at Michelle's and it was like how it used to be, pure bliss.

The morning we set off for London for me to go into hiding – they like you to go into hiding for a few days before the show – it felt done and finished. I was about to begin a new chapter in my life, I said goodbye to Michelle and my son and my chaperone,

Ali, who had come and picked me up.

One of the first things she did was ask for my phone. Now Big Brother didn't know anything about Laurie, and I didn't feel like I needed to talk about it. So I ran off down the road so she couldn't hear me, and it was one last call to the turd in the tin. His words were priceless:

"Helen, you're mad doing this, no one will like you, they're just going to slate you became of what you've done in the past, you'll be out in a week," to which I replied: "Fuck it, a week's a week." Laurie said, "Don't let this change you, and I'll see you in a few weeks." I thought, "No you won't, pal..."

In my mind I was single and happy, but I knew full well he'd be telling his prison mates that his bird was going on Big Brother and he'd be watching.

The we drove off to Surrey and shacked up in the most gorgeous little cottage, with no TV, no radio, nothing. I wasn't allowed any contact with the outside world. I watched Cold Feet about seventy times and listened to Oasis, and drove Ali around the bend with my need for pampering. We went shopping but she was so strict on me talking to people, and bollocked me for sneaking into a newsagent to peep at the papers. I loved it all, I didn't feel nervous, and it was like the best adventure of my life – and this was only the build-up!

I got to the hotel next to the studios and my hair extensions had arrived. There was a hair salon in the hotel, but the people working there were the biggest bunch of stuck-up arseholes you'll ever meet. I took the extensions and asked if they could be coloured, but first the reception girl ignored me, and then she was rude to me, so it escalated pretty quickly into a full-blown row. I was meant to be getting my hair coloured and cut there, too.

I ended up telling them to screw their appointment. They had my coat and refused to give it to me unless I paid.

You couldn't make it up – I'm meant to be keeping a low profile but here I am being barricaded in a salon, being threatened with the police because I refuse to pay for an arsehole to do my hair. My chaperone hadn't seen this side to me and panicked: "Helen, I'll see if the producers will pay for the cancellation." This enraged me even more: "NO, they're getting nothing, if anyone pays on my behalf I'll go mad."

They let me go and security took me to my bedroom, Ali rang Michelle, who then spoke to me, the voice of reason. I was so worked up, just because I'm going on a programme doesn't mean to say I have to be any different than I would be any other day. One of the producers came into my room and explained how I'd have to pay for the cancellation of the hair app. I couldn't believe this was happening, hours before I was about to go on telly, I said nicely: "Sorry, I know it's a predicament for you, but I'm not paying anything, and nobody's going to pay on my behalf either."

I'm not sure what happened, and my hair was about forty shades of brown, but the BB countdown was on...

Most people who know me know how confident I am as a person, however, my confidence was about to be tested more than ever.

The night came for the big entrance and I took a wobble, it probably didn't help that I'd necked half a bottle of wine to myself. I was sat in the car with my chaperone and a driver and I was told to put on a blindfold. Now the only time I've appreciated being blindfolded is when I'm tied to a bed, thinking of England; I couldn't keep it on, I was shouted at by the crew because I kept peeping through it, then I went into panic mode and said, "I can't wear this thing, it's making me anxious, even more than I already am."

We arrived and the car stopped, a researcher opened the door and leaned in: "Come on Helen, it's your turn."

I've got to give it to them, they're great at their job and don't put up with any shit. Before I could object any further I was at the top of the steps, stood behind the Big Brother eye.

The researcher hugged me, and said: "Chop chop, Helen, go and have the best summer of your life."

I could hear my voice on the VT, and it was going through me. "My name's Helen, and I like white wine". Why the hell did I say that? My voice alone would get me kicked off, I decided. But as I tried to pull back the doors opened, and I was blinded by the lights and deafened by the boos of the crowd, but knew I couldn't turn back now.

I felt so vulnerable walking along that stage.

The minute I was in, it went quiet, and the whole layout just felt so homely and safe.

In a way, I had an advantage over the other contestants. I knew I couldn't really go any lower in the public's opinion, so I could just be myself, and what was the worst that could happen? They still wouldn't like me.

I had hardened myself to public opinion.

I was so excited to meet Emma Willis, she always seemed like the loveliest and most gorgeous presenter, but over my time on the show I really changed my mind – I thought she was frosty and biased. With her killer looks and sweet TV persona, I can see why she's done as well as she has, and well played. In the TV industry you need to be savvy, but Rylan was a much better person for the job in my mind. He has a genuine interest for the show and the housemates, he watches every single second, in the same way that Rachel Riley has an interest in maths. Rylan takes his job so seriously and makes sure he gives everyone a chance. He's your ultimate professional presenter, I absolutely adore how this guy has no doubt made a lot of money, but he's still the exact same person from the X Factor where he bawled his eyes out like a bitch.

CHAPTER TWELVE

B ig Brother is a game, but it depends how you look at it: the only time I thought I was participating in a game was when I was taking part in a task or challenge; I never once thought I was going to win in this house, I was just there for a bit of fun, I had no tactics, no preconceptions, I was just bloody happy to be in that house. With my personality, I thought there wasn't a chance I would win, I did get lucky though, and I was immune from nominations from the start and throughout the whole process, no one could ever nominate me because another contestant, Pauline, chose me to give me immunity throughout the whole process. So after being in there five minutes I thought: "Shit, I'm already in the final, I'm gonna be here for weeks." Pauline chose me because she recognised me the minute I walked through the door and she thought I'd get a chance, bless her.

She later told me she chose me because she didn't think people would give me a chance on the outside, that'd take a while and more than a few episodes for the public to see what she sees, so I guess I was one lucky cow.

Hand on heart, I had one of the best years of meeting people: even people that I would never in a million years speak to in my normal walk of life, they all had a story to tell, everyone was interesting in their own little way.

As soon I walked in and the doors closed I felt at home straightaway. I settled in very quickly – very bloody quickly from what my friends said: they were all sat at home, hands on heads, watching me drink wine with anticipation, worried what I'd say or do if someone arrived who I didn't click with.

The first couple of nights on the show, I was in my element, buzzing to be around people just as chatty and outspoken as me.

I thought from the beginning my relationship would go one

way or another with Mark Byron, I thought either get he'd get on my nerves or we'd bounce off each other; he soon became one of my best mates in the house; I also thought Steve would be a snob for someone of his age, and to be as successful as him, but he was so down-to-earth, Steve's family were like a second home to me when I came out of Big Brother. I've never met a warmer, more loving family, it's not often you meet someone that's good through and through, that's Steve and all his family.

Out of the whole experience I recollect two, maybe three days where I was really low and desperately wanted to see my son and friends. People asked why I didn't talk about my son more on the show, but for me our relationship is a very personal thing, it's not something to go into detail about to a room full of strangers – or to be broadcast to a nation.

When the intensity kicks in and boredom, arguments start, people get snappy and sensitive, and those few days I felt like I was trapped and not able to be myself, because everything I said or did was being misinterpreted.

I got branded a bully by the public, and I see why, from the outside looking in when the whole story wasn't being shown.

There was a female housemate in particular who really peed me off. She entered the house having claimed she had no fags, when I had 250 and a couple of the lads had cigs too. We all smoked each other's and shared them with her. Then a couple of weeks in we failed a task for the shopping budget, so weren't awarded any tobacco, then this housemate revealed she had bags of tobacco in her case for rollups, but wouldn't share it with us. Thinking back it's not a big deal, but at the time I actually wanted to swing for her for being such a selfish twat. I was a dick with her for the next couple of weeks, any given opportunity to be a cow with her I was. I'm not proud of that but then I don't like tight-arses who claim poverty then turn out to be sly.

I clashed with quite a few of the housemates, because as time goes on you really start to see people's true colours, now given that my true colours are on display within minutes of people meeting me, that's hard for someone like me to contend with and it got my back up, A LOT. On the outside I'd walk away from people like this and give them the cold shoulder, but there's no escaping in there.

You'd see people working the camera, being fake for the purpose of winning the public's vote. I couldn't and wouldn't sit around that carry-on, I spent three months more or less calling out fakeness whilst thinking the public won't like me because I can't be fake. I shout a lot, I swear like a sailor, but then I'm also the one who cooks everyone's meals every day and does all the washing. I was kind of the agony aunt too for a lot of them – proper blowing my own trumpet here, aren't I?! The show didn't present these sides of me, though. They know the role they want you to be when you enter, and it wasn't long before I was branded the house bitch/villain.

I met a guy called Ash in there, who was the best form of a rebound from Laurie. I thought he was Swedish, as he was tall, tanned, with long hair, and stood out to me massively. We did many tasks or games (I loved them) and in one Ash got asked: "Which girl in the house do you find most attractive?" Everyone giggled, they knew where this question was going. I actually shit myself when he said my name as I'd been so out of touch and on a roller coaster with my ex for so long I hadn't considered any other guy. But you know when you're about nine years old and you want to act all cool in front of a boy you like? I was totally out of my comfort zone and started acting weirdly around him.

Then one night we played spin the bottle. As usual a couple of us had robbed the store cupboard blind so we could drink all the alcohol, I ended up a little bit drunk let's just say, and surprise surprise, me and Ash were dared to kiss. Bloody hell, we sound like a bunch of twelve-year-olds.

We kissed, I sat back, then it sank in what I'd just done in front of a nation watching. I'll be honest, I felt a bit shit for Laurie, he can have a taste of his own medicine but on a bigger scale. That was the last time I thought about him.

Me and Ash shared a bed for the rest of the summer and that's that, no we didn't shag like so many people have asked. I might be a horny dog, but banging on TV... not cool. For me that crosses a line.

My fear about going to the loo on camera stuck with me, and I didn't go for a number two for two weeks. I got stage fright. I couldn't go because of the cameras and I made myself ill in the end. Producers gave me fibre gel and peppermint tablets to help me along and when I eventually really needed to go I put a sock over the camera...!

The only time my outside life made an appearance in my Big Brother bubble is when I was called out as the police had apparently driven to the studio from up north and wanted to see me. They wouldn't explain why to the Big Brother staff so I absolutely shit myself, and assumed it was to do with Laurie.

There was three of them but it turned out it was to do with a minor car accident I'd had a while before. I was relieved, but I'm not really sure why they felt the need to find me while I was in the house, I obviously wasn't going anywhere... Couldn't they have spoken to me when I came out? I think they just wanted to be nosey.

I grew close to a couple of the housemates who I still to this day adore to pieces. You do genuinely believe there is a strong bond with people, until the end of the show starts to make an appearance. Ash distanced himself from me because he thought I'd spoil his chances of winning, ha, well that went tits up. But I was fine with that, and didn't feel any animosity towards him as it became a game. The last couple of weeks people really started to show their (ugly) true colours, yet I remained the same old gobshite I'd been since day one.

Both myself and another girl were in the final, I can't honestly say she got to that position by herself, there was zero personality really and in the end I was tired of going head to head with her, but I genuinely wanted this girl to do well in life. She was younger and kind of reminded me of the annoying year seven that you just had to ignore at times.

Anyway, it was the final and I was sat on the sofa, if you remember the night I was sat right on the edge, I thought as soon as the public got their hands on me, I was gone. If you watched the show you'll realise that when it got to the final night I was bricking myself, I thought I'd be the first to go out of the six of us left. I thought Emma would come on and say, "…and the sixth person to be evicted from the Big Brother house is Helen". I was waiting for that, at a push fifth. When she announced that me and Ashley were runners-up and we were the only two left in that house, I couldn't get my head around it. I thought the minute the public wanted to get me out, they would. I thought they would have only shown me arguing, and nothing about me being nice.

Anyway, we were waiting for Emma to announce the winner when I heard, "Helen, you are the Big Brother winner!" I couldn't fucking believe it, I was shaking, I could not believe I was coming out of this show the winner. Big Brother was saying, "Sit down, Helen", but I said I can't and I kept walking around, I was like a raving looney, pacing the living room up and down, it felt like a dream, but then it felt so real because the feeling was just so overwhelming. I walked up the stairs like a charging elephant, I went in a size eight and came out a size twelve after eating a loaf of fresh bread every day; my dress didn't fit, my shoes were awful, my dress was too short and I had Captain Hook ringlets from the hairdresser all over my head (any of my current or previous hairdressers will sympathise with the hairdresser that did my hair that day, it's all about the bounce, not the ringlets), but fuck it, I had just won Big Brother. I still don't know how, but hey, I won't and didn't complain...!

I had my interview with Emma and then I looked over and saw Michelle. Emma didn't think I was a deserving winner, it was written all over her face. Watching the worst and best bits back were equally as toe-curling, but I didn't regret a single thing, I still don't. I sat talking to Emma about all the ups and downs and the housemates, all I could think about was I could go backstage in ten minutes and have a glass of wine with my bestie, I might have wanted to talk a bit more but I got the impressions Emma didn't want to talk to me much, I'd just won a hundred grand. Get me the fuck outta here, I thought.

The public never cease to amaze me though, in what they believe they are watching; when it comes to editing the show it's a big job, Big Brother is a show where the team have to watch usually very boring people sit around all day and play a few games then take snippets from the 'best' parts of the day and create a scene; things aren't always what they seem. I often get asked, did it not anger you when you found out Big Brother had stitched you up on certain scenes, for example showing just me to be the villain; the truth is no, what's the point in getting angry over something I can't change, and even more important, I signed up to?

It's like being a rat in a laboratory, or a pawn that can be moved around or used as and when the puppet-master feels like pulling your strings – don't get me wrong, I'm really grateful for lovely comments and emails over the years since Big Brother, but if I could urge any of you lovely people to do one thing it would be DON'T TAKE IT TOO SERIOUSLY, IT'S A GAME. Careful editing makes a programme for you to watch, and that's all.

Michelle was so tiny, she looked amazing, but she'd lost so much weight. We aren't normally a hugging friendship duo, but she clung onto me and said, "Don't ever leave me again." This wasn't like her, those words wouldn't usually have come out of her mouth, I thought. She said she needed to talk to me, but privately; we went into the toilets and she told me that one of the girls who I'd left in charge of the shop had basically made the girls' lives in the shop, and Michelle's life, living hell while I was away. She sold stories on me and the shop had nearly closed; Michelle had been handling everything while I was away, including my son. I'm forever grateful to her for that. I told her not to worry and I'd sort it, and thank you so much for looking after everything.

Because I'd won I had so many people wanting to talk to me, Michelle just told me to go and do my thing while she waited at the bar. So I was speaking to journalists, other cast members, researchers of the show and the producer. There was only one other boy that I would want to see and speak to that night, and that was my son.

We went to my hotel room and got leathered. Michelle showed me a banner she'd made with "Helen to WIN" coloured on it.

She was very proud of it, and we were jumping around saying how exciting it was that I had just won Big Brother.

Then a friend called, and said, "Congratulations on winning, you were great Helen, don't worry about Laurie and this kid with this bird, though."

"What?"

It turned out that the night that I kissed Ash, Laurie had put up a picture of a baby on social media that he had behind my back. The kid was a few months old; he had a son who he also called Laurie; there are no other words to describe my feelings but numb.

"I didn't want you to find out tonight, not after you were on such a high," Michelle said. You could see it had killed her, and it had burdened her for weeks, this piece of shit had not only just caused grief, he'd stolen money off me, lived off the back of me and my son, and he had now reduced my friend to tears.

"Fuck him," I said, and we ignored it, carrying on laughing and catching up with what I had missed.

Michelle showed me her son's birthday party and told me how well my son was doing; three months was a long time to catch up on and I was just so excited to be there with Michelle.

Michelle, bless her, didn't show me anything in the press or papers, unless it was something funny, because anything negative was completely blown out of proportion; the next day after winning Big Brother I had tons of press; it's quite funny, Amy, one of the researchers, came over to the hotel with two massive binders full of press. She said she had never had to deal with a housemate that had so many newspaper clippings and press, and she told me to enjoy! She said I'd been in the papers every day. I've never looked at the binder to this day, it's in my garage, I never ever felt the need to.

The support from people afterwards was unreal, I'd been expecting people to be vile towards me once I left; this didn't happen, to be honest I found it uncomfortable how positive the public were towards me. I did a couple of charity events and I had kids coming having pics with me, I was like whhhhy do they know who I am, these innocent beings? My own kid didn't watch any of it apart from me winning, why do these young girls know who I am, they shouldn't, but whatever, not my kids, not my prob.

I was told to stay down in London and to "strike whilst the iron's hot", but I didn't. I didn't want to mingle with anyone from the TV world and I didn't want to be famous, so I went back to Bolton two days later.

Except, I arrived home to find a trashed house. A girl who used to come into the salon, who I thought was sweet, broke down into tears to my nail girl a week before I was heading to Big Brother. Her mum had thrown her out and was making life hell for her. I have absolutely no idea why I did this, but I messaged her on Facebook telling her to come to my house.

Cut a long story short, this timid ginger girl who you'd think butter wouldn't melt, told me she had nowhere to go and felt trapped and depressed. I knew how it felt to have parents like hers and I'll always empathise with that situation, so I offered her my home whilst I went away.

I kitted out the spare room and made it all homely and cute, but whilst I was in the big bro house she had parties, shagged in my bed, and brought a flea-bag cat into the house that ruined my new carpets; the house was trashed, full of cat crap and piss. It wasn't liveable, but when I threatened to smash her face in she rang the police. Guess who got threatened with a caution? The good ol' justice system, aye?!

I moved into Michelle's for about three months whilst the house was done up, and tried to go back to normal life, but it was bloody hard. I learnt that although my nearest and dearest were happy I'd won, a lot of people in my home town were just pissed off about it – the brass that won the public's vote, must've been a fix, she must've shagged the producer, bla bla bla, you name it I was accused of it. I realised a long time ago before Big Brother days that people actually WANT to not like me, fair do's, you can't please everyone and why would you want to?!

I received a phone call from my son's school at seven-fifteen a.m. one morning about graffiti on the whole of my son's school and the bus stops in the surrounding area. My son's name, along with "His mum is a whore …. brass". Luckily it was all removed by eight-thirty a.m.

What kind of person tries to hurt a nine-year-old child? Thankfully he never saw the graffiti, but he has heard other things and luckily he always comes directly to me. I told him as he has got older that I used to do something that might cause people to be really hurtful and say nasty things to him; I didn't want him to retaliate and I told him, you've got to realise if anybody says anything to you it's because they're weak, and he replied with the best possible response: "Yeah, I'm not bothered if anyone says anything, well, that's about my mum isn't it, not me, speak to her if you've got a problem." I just laughed and gave him a cuddle – he's literally nothing like I was as a child, if he was any more laid-back he'd be asleep, he's an amazing boy.

I loved being at Michelle's. Michelle's Lee is lovely, he's such a good egg, he welcomed me and my son into their house, he's a great dad too, and a fab husband, I love him and Michelle so much. I will always defend men when people say all men are the same, I would like to say that Lee is close to one hundred per cent perfect. Ralph, my little godson, was only four at the time, he would wake me up each morning to have breakfast with him, I sat there and watched all the kids play outside together, I would sit on the couch with Michelle having a brew, it was just amazing, it was such bliss.

Two weeks after Big Brother I took most of the housemates on a little holiday to Ibiza. There were nine of us out of sixteen that went, we had made a pinkie promise in the house that whoever won would take everyone to Ibiza, I stuck to it and took us all. Although I only speak to two members in that house these days, most turned out to be conniving bastards. Some of them have shown their true colours since, but you can still have good memories with people that in the end turn out to be shit-heads. I still don't regret it, Ibiza is my favourite place in the world, and still an experience to add to my life.

Two other housemates who I'd got on really well with whilst in the house decided to sell some bullshit story to the papers about me, for £250. They were meant to be staying in the villa, but not after that. They rang Ash's phone whilst we were chilling one day at the pool. I took over the phone call: "The papers are lying, Helen."

Yeah, ok, likely story. I can't deny how much I enjoyed floating around on my lilo in my 60-foot pool sipping a G and T, telling these two to kiss my arse.

Turns out that a lot of the housemates, when they got out and learned who I was and about my colourful past, tried to sell so many lies. I wouldn't mind but you could sell facts on me and the papers would've had a bloody field day, no need to fabricate!

Ash had backed off from me in the last few days of the Big

Brother house, things just fizzled out, but on the outside he did ask if we could go on a date, so we did, and we had a really nice time, we got on really well and I enjoyed myself. We went back to his and we were sat on the couch chilling and listening to music, when he took a picture of us both and put it on my Twitter, it was one of the most retweeted pictures on Twitter of me ever, actually. He captioned it something like "Chilling with my boy", and I don't speak like this, but he tweeted it. I remember being pretty pissed, thinking why had he put "Chilling with my boy" when I don't use words like that, I would never describe cuddling with a guy I'm about to shag as chilling … whatever, no harm done though, I did actually look quite nice on the pic, even after three bottles of wine and a couple of brandies.

We started seeing each other a lot but he started to make out to everyone that I was all over him and I wasn't. It didn't take me long to realise he had nothing to really offer me, he was another one with no work ethic, he had no ambition or drive. We did have a few good nights out in Manchester, we dated on and off for a while, he was just there really, he became my friend more than anything else, there were just little things that didn't work, like the sex wasn't dirty enough, for someone as good-looking as him, you'd think he's dead confident in the bedroom, but he wasn't; it was a fling, and a good rebound, Ash was a party guy for me and at that time that was perfect; we'd been on a night out, one of our few, and I'm probably not the only girl, when you've been out with a guy you're seeing, shagging, dating, whatever you wanna call it, but the best bit is getting home and wanting to rip each other's clothes off, shagging, drinking, talking, but mainly shagging.

It wasn't like that with Ash, I thought it might be me coming across as some kind of sexual fiend that he wasn't used to, but his recent ex and previous ex both got in contact with me when I did a column to say I wasn't imagining things, he was just limp in the bedroom with everyone. I was hoping for a drink-fuelled after-party full of filthy sex that didn't happen, one quick how's-your-father was all I got and he started to nod off again.

I'm pretty sure I'm speaking for lots of girls that when you've had a drink one bit of hanky panky is not exactly enough, it should be exciting; we'd only just started seeing each other. He was being so grumpy I thought, fuck it, I would just play with myself, so I got my vibrator and did it myself, while he was lying next to me. He asked me what the noise was and then he ripped the covers off us, anyone would think Jimmy Savile was lying next to him, the way he looked at me and the vibrator. Well, this is awkward I thought, between the noise of the vibrator sounding like a small cement mixer and the huffing and puffing coming from this choirboy, I seriously started to question: did I need therapy, or did he need to seek help about his libido?

Even when me and my ex were at loggerheads, if I'd turned the vibrator on next to him in bed he was like a rat up a drainpipe. Michelle said, "I don't understand why this person is in your life Helen, he's not good in bed, he already owes you loads of money, and you're not really into him." She told me to fuck him off, she was right, so I texted him saying can we have a chat?

That kind of seriousness does not sit well with someone like Ash. I went around and said we should just be friends and stop sleeping with each other; he mutually agreed, thank fuck, we stayed in contact as friends after that and then like a fucking idiot I lent him £3,000 when he called me asking for help. He came to me with a sob story that he needed help, he was sick of no one ever giving him a chance and he wanted his own business, the bank wouldn't even open a bank account for him so I opened it in both our names, and lent him the money. I then totally forgot about it, I trusted him, he never gave me a reason not to, I didn't want to fuck him but he'd always been nice to me. I didn't think he would abuse what I'd done for him or what I'd given him.

A few months down the line I was in the bank and I thought, "I'll just get a mini statement for that account." I was intrigued. All of it had gone, the lot, I looked at the statement and it was just rammed with transactions like Reiss Clothing, Neighbourhood (a bar in Manchester), Topman, clothes here, dinner there, everything had gone and in fact it was in the minus, so he'd left me in the red as well. I had lent him that money for a business opportunity, not for fucking shit, I called him and I told him he had twenty-four hours to get that money back to me, otherwise he was going in my next column in the paper that I was writing at the time, and I would expose him.

He didn't believe I would do it and tried doing the whole reverse psychology tactic, "I'll just tell everyone you're obsessed with me and you only wanted the money back because you finished with me." I said good luck with that one, I have every message you sent me screenshot in case something like this would happen, he didn't listen though and he didn't give me the money, so I destroyed him in the article and put the screenshots in it.

CHAPTER THIRTEEN

I was single and concentrating on my own life and work now, but God, I was quickly finding the hair and beauty industry isn't for me. I adore tattooing eyebrows, I ADORE my clients, but the industry itself actually made me ill. Coming off a TV show and then within weeks returning to a salon – aka the witches' coven – wasn't the best.

Alarm bells went off when I took the girls who worked in my salon for dinner, a couple of nights before I went into hiding. It was a lovely restaurant, but they were loud, rude, and embarrassing.

After I came out of the house, a client messaged me explaining how she wouldn't be returning to the salon because she couldn't bear to listen to them slag me off any longer. I wanted to know what the problem was, so called a staff meeting, politely asking if anyone had any issues, did anyone have anything to say about me being away for so long, had I upset anyone, "No babe, just glad to have you back," "Don't be daft, we knew you were gonna win." Tongues so far up my arse they could taste what I'd had for my dinner – sorry to be crass! Nobody did the decent thing and said about any problem they had that could have been ironed out.

A few days later I returned to the salon with Michelle, grabbed some sun bed tokens and went upstairs to the sunbed room, after being greeted by the sweetest (fakest) workers downstairs. I popped the token in the sunbed and quietly opened the door so I could listen to them all go in tooth and nail on me.

"She takes the piss waltzing in like that, she's only here for the rent."

Oh, yes. How dare I pick up the rent for my business...?

Anyway, this didn't last much longer. I started being a twat on the sly, making false bookings so I knew they'd have to come in and wait about for invisible people, pulling silly pranks just for my own amusement.

The girls eventually closed up and posted the key, then set up a shop a few miles up the road. I didn't chase them up, but closed the salon for two weeks, sat back and thought good luck setting up a business when you've all shown each other you're liars, onto the new recruits.

I took on new staff, but they were equally as toxic, so I decided my time in the business was done. I moved on – making sure everything I'd been so careful to do up in the building was ripped out again before I left. No one else was going to benefit from my hard work!

I'd never consider opening a salon again, as very few women can be happy for one another. Where I work now, the lady who owns it is miles younger than me, which some girls would hate but I couldn't give two shits. She's fair, she says if there's an issue, lets you get on with your work, and that's all I need. I like to earn my money, pack up and piss off.

I was finding it more difficult than ever to get remotely close to any guy, in both emotional and sexual ways. I suppose you would say I'm back to square one where I was years ago before the escorting, when I found it very easy to plod along and keep a barrier up. In a way they've been bliss, in the respect that I haven't had to cry, worry or be controlled by any male influence, I say "bliss" and I genuinely mean that. I've taken these four years to find myself, love myself, and treat myself exactly how any girl should be treated.

My friends say I'm fussy, I'm not, I just don't have the time for any bullshit. Although to be fair I don't let many people close enough to find out if they're full of it or not – it's less risky, and easier, to just shut off. A huge fear of mine is being lied to and someone laughing at me behind my back.

One thing I massively miss is sex, though. Sex for me is a huge thing, but now I'm that bit older and I've had my fingers burnt and I've experienced being in the public eye, I can't just go out and have a fling – not that there is anything wrong with that, if that's what you choose to do with your life. I sometimes wish I was able to go out, fancy a guy and think yeah, I'd go home with him tonight, but I mentally and physically can't do that anymore, so I'm now Ann Summers' favourite customer.

I told my friends about how much I needed sex, to the point that it really gets me down sometimes and I've had to speak to a therapist about it. I had a photoshoot coming up in London and they said, "Helen, just go out tonight and sleep with someone. You're never gonna see them again, don't even exchange numbers, just go out and have a good time." Now half of me was saying yes, while half of me was saying no, I probably should have stuck with the latter. I was out in London after my shoot, having a bloody good night actually, when I met some guys who were (seemed) really nice; the drinks were flowing, it was a heavy, boozy night filled with good conversation, which let's face it people don't know how to talk any more, they're always on social media, so this was going well. I spent a good few hours talking to this fittie; not once did he flash his watch, not once did he flash the sole of his shoes, and not once did he try and act flash about what he did for a job. We spoke about his son, which I think endeared me even more to him, and we spoke about travel, something again I love to talk about, so this guy was ticking all the boxes, especially for just a one-night stand.

To cut a long story short, I'm drunk, he's drunk, it was like the ideal cheese-on-toast film, driving around London in a black cab, smooching away.

Off we trotted to the hotel room, we were all over each other in the lift, I remember absolutely tingling from head to toe and inside thinking "I actually fancy this guy," and I hadn't fancied anyone since my ex properly, but still reminding myself that this was just a one-night stand, which I think is good to have in mind as you don't allow yourself to be too flirtatious (although this will never be my strong point, guys often tell me I'm really hard to read ... good).

It doesn't take a genius to work out what happened with an hour of us getting in the hotel room: things progressed pretty quickly, when I say quickly, from pouring some drinks, talking shit and the usual steamy routine, the neck got kissed, the ear got nibbled, the knickers got dropped, then BOOM, cameras ready, prepare to flash – he'd Snapchatted me, but the dozy fuck forgot to turn the flash off. I quickly turned around and shouted, "What the fuck was that?" I went into panic mode, I couldn't actually even speak, bearing in mind I thought the Snapchat had already been sent out online. He started flapping, saying, "Helen, look, I promise I haven't sent it. Look."

I just sat there with a glum expression on my face. I didn't believe he hadn't sent it. I was still puzzled as to why someone would ever do this. The first thing I said to him level-headedly was, "Hang on a minute, we spent the best part of four to five hours talking about our kids, so you know I have a child, but more to the point you have a son and you spoke to me about how you have such a good relationship with your son's mum, who is also a single mum, so how would you feel if your son's mum was getting fucked and a piece of shit like you sent a video out to the world?"

He was actually gobsmacked and froze for a second after I said this; now this guy you could see had the potential to be a cocky, arrogant arsehole – well, he was an arsehole for doing that, but he quickly backtracked and said, "I never thought about it like that, I'm so sorry, it was just a laugh, my friends didn't believe I was with you."

So he'd spent all night with me but didn't mention he knew who I was; it hit the pit of my stomach when he said those words: this is a sad reality of today's society, everything is Snapchatted, people who have been on reality TV for some reason are looked at differently than your everyday Joe.

I never have and never will, no matter what media work I do, ever want to be treated differently than anybody else.

I might be naïve, but I think telling him to put the boot on the other foot by asking him if his child's mum was exploited for all to see getting shagged, how would it make him feel? For anyone thinking, why am I bothered, my son knows what I did for a living, well yes, but he's never encountered or seen anything to do with me and a man besides my ex; last thing I wanted him to see is a video like that. It's one thing people slinging mud at me but to drag kids into any situation is just wrong on every level, and social media can do that easily these days.

I decided after this it was too much hassle finding someone to have sex with. I know my friends were encouraging me to go out and have some fun, but I couldn't be arsed with the trouble that could come with it.

Then I met a certain Mr IT boy (model) at an awards party, the guy in question is a well-known British Lothario (well, so he thinks); he came over to speak to me, and certainly had the charm and the chat and I could see why he gets the ladies. I thought he was fit but we just chatted and nothing more happened. I didn't see him for a while after that, and although he did message me a few times on Twitter, I didn't message back.

Out of the blue he got in touch saying he was in Manchester, and asked: "Helen where are you?" I was meant to go out with my mates but on the day it got cancelled, so I replied, "I'm at home, why?"

"Come and see me, I'm at the Malmaison in Manchester."

I thought about my friends encouraging me to go and meet someone, so before I could think any more on it, I bit the bullet.

I got in my car and drove to the hotel. He'd sent me the room number but it was the wrong one. I went to reception and said, "I'm here to see my friend, I think his room number is …" to which she replied, "He's not in that room," I said, "Can you please ring whichever room number he's in and let him know I'm here."

My blood was boiling at this point; it's just not the scenario you want in life. I actually started leaving the hotel because I could see the receptionist's eyes burning into my skull, but as I was leaving he rang. "Babe, just wait there, the waitress is gonna bring you up with some drinks, just wait." I went back in, dragging my feet, and the waitress asked what I wanted to drink, I needed a stiff one at this point – and I didn't mean his dick. Off we trotted up the stairs, the waitress talking to me like my new best friend; this was all very weird, maybe he smashed her earlier on, I wouldn't be surprised.

He opened the door and gave me a kiss; it didn't take me thirty seconds to enter the room and realise he was talking shit and he was shaking, typical bloke, CANNOT handle his drug intake and booze, in fact I think I've only met three males in my life that don't turn into complete tosspots when under the influence.

I was trying to talk to him, it felt like we were having a therapy session, he kept saying "Who've you told you're here?" I said "No one," which was the truth. We sat down and started talking, but his manner kept changing, like Jekyll and Hyde; he would ask me questions about my life but I would restrain myself, as I didn't actually want to tell him anything.

He begged me to get some stuff dropped off to the room; he was getting flappy, pacing the room, and I replied, "I don't know anyone around here."

I was laughing, but nervously as he seemed so edgy and unpredictable. I guess that beats boring, so it's probably why I stuck around – well, that and the bottle and a half of wine I'd sunk.

He got about four grams bought to the hotel by this young local weedy lad, who I guess was a local Joey, the guy who sells direct to the customers. I felt really uncomfortable with the way he spoke to this lad, all about his appearance and girls, but not giving this guy a chance to speak, it was a bizarre situation.

I was hesitant to butt in because I thought, are these two friends? Is this some kind of weird bromance they've got going on, where one is the dominator and he's just this weedy Joey that takes shit from him?

Eventually the Joey asked for his money, he just turned, looked at us both in his drug-fuelled mess and said "There's me card" – he flicked his bank card at the guy and told him to go to the ATM machine.

"What are you doing?" I asked. "You can't speak to people like that, you can't be sending him to find an ATM with your card."

The lad picked up the card and said, "Don't worry love, I'll just go to the one downstairs."

"No you won't, he can put some clothes on and go and draw it out himself, you're not his slave."

It was becoming such an awkward situation that I figured I had to nip it in the bud and jokingly said to the lad, "Do you have a chip'n'pin machine, if not I'll do you a transfer."

The lad gave me his details and I pinged over just under a couple of hundred quid and off he went.

Not even five seconds later the door was closed, and he stood up and said, "Who do you think you are, girl? You don't act like that in my company, when you're in my company you're my girl."

I thought he was referring to me transferring the money and bailing out his skint ass, but he was actually referring to the reference I had put on the transaction. He actually accused me of putting my phone number as the reference for the transaction. Paranoid doesn't even begin to come into it.

I started laughing: "Are you for real? You're actually deranged."

I got up to go and get my coat and handbag, when his attitude switched: "No, no, babes, what are you doing? You gotta understand, a lot of girls have fucked with my head."

"This is not my problem, I don't care about other girls, you're boring me."

He told me I didn't understand what it was like to be him: "I'm in a dark place and I can't get out."

Yes, I'm frosty and I can be cold towards people, but even though this poor excuse of a man had gone from an eight to a zero in my estimation, I couldn't and wouldn't walk out straightaway when someone says something like that. I sat back down and asked him why did he think it was okay to speak to people like that, and did he realise how messed up it is, thinking there was something going on between me and the runner-bean drug dealer. He went on to say he was so used to girls disrespecting him and cheating on him – although I was trying my hardest to empathise.

I'm quite good at reading people, and this didn't feel like a genuine "Please listen to me, I've had it bad", but more of a "I've realised I've been a dick, and what excuse can I pluck from the sky to redeem what an arsehole I've just been."

Then BOOM, the ultimate X Factor-audition-style sob-line came up: his late dad.

"I'm totally fucked since losing my dad in the limelight to alcohol, the pressure is constantly on, they've even got a suite in this hotel reminding me of him."

It just didn't sit well with me. I know people who have gone through really dark times – me included – but I don't treat people the way he just had. But it was soon obvious he didn't want to be told I thought he was wrong, or to hear any advice on what to do.

So instead we carried on drinking – I'd sunk at least two bottles of wine by now – and ended up having sex. On the way to the hotel I'd been looking forward to that, because I thought he'd tick all the boxes.

I couldn't have been more wrong.

He's a good-looking guy who's completely ruined himself with an egotistical, paranoid, nasty attitude. The sex wasn't anything to shout about, I do remember he was hung like a small bull and I thought this would have kept me hanging around a lot longer, maybe at least some good sex would have extinguished the fact this guy is completely not right, but it didn't; we had sex once, I pretended he'd hit me in the right spot and fell asleep, pretty sure I was having an out-of-body experience because this is not how I usually act, if I like a guy's company and they turn me on they know about it.

We were in bed for about eleven p.m. (rock'n'roll!). I remember I woke up about one a.m. feeling really hazy, looking at my phone and drinking a ton of water to try and sober myself up, I text my friend Becky who was out in Manchester that night, saying ring my phone at four a.m., saying you need me, I'll explain later, just make sure you ring me. I lay there from one a.m. to four a.m., clock-watching, then voilà, ring ring, Becky saved the day; we had our 'false emergency' on the phone, although I doubt he was even listening, he was asleep. I got my shit together, but then he sat up slightly in bed and said "What you doing, babe? Come back to bed." I said, "I can't, I gotta go, I got work at eight" (like I'd be doing someone's eyebrows at eight a.m. on a Sunday morning). He said, "Okay babes, I'm so glad you came over, I'll text you tomorrow." I gave him one more very confused look and pondered the idea of ringing psychiatric help for him.

I wouldn't mind if I'd given a good performance and put the effort in, but I can consciously say I now know what lads mean when they say, "She lay there like a sack of spuds." I may as well have had Mr Bean on top of me; the filthy Lothario I had thought I was finally meeting, who I'd seen a lot on TV and in magazines looking fit, turned out to be none other than a bell-end that needs a 24-hour psychiatric nurse to guide him in life.

Goes to show that looks mean nothing and I should probably have carried on with the celibacy. As I always joke to my friends, he might be sporting a todger like a tiger bread but his personality (when drunk) is equivalent to a mouldy loaf!

I thought that would be the last I heard from him after my piss-poor performance and my lack of empathy to his baloney, but how sweet (rolls eyes): he texted me the next day to say what a nice time he had; this guy is seriously cuckoo, if that's his idea of a good night he needs to get out more, it was one of the worst encounters I've ever had, and I've had a few.

The fling between me and this guy was 'magically' leaked to the papers, who ran a story on it. When I asked him how the hell they knew, he replied "You tell me" – that old chestnut. I know who I'd told about it and I knew they wouldn't have been gossiping.

Little did he know I know someone who works in the accounts department whose job is to pay tip-offs, and oh yes, it turns out that sooo many people in the cringe reality tv world who all act like bum chums are screwing one another over for a quick buck.

Anyway, turns out this guy's agent tips them off at times, which most likely meant he was behind this story too. I know what it's like being stuck for cash, so I hope that £500 got them a few round of drinks and some peanuts!

About two weeks later a good friend of mine texted me saying "Helen, you in the Malmaison with your model mate?" A friend of my mate's had texted him saying that Mr Lothario was there in the Malmaison Manchester with some brunette. His mate took a pic of the bird, turns out it's only a girl I know; I immediately had a field day and texted him saying "Do you take all your brunette bitches to the Malmaison?" (Laughing emoji.) "I hope you've emptied your piggy bank for tonight's date, don't be having her paying for your narcotics." To which he replied "Lol, what do you mean, where are you?"

They finished in the bar and got up and went towards the lift. I was having a three-way convo with my friend's mate on text, who thought it would be funny to follow him to the lift and update me on the goss. They all got in and he's gone to floor three. I texted again, "Oh, floor three are we tonight, did I get the lucky suite, she's been demoted." He texted me back again at this point saying, "Where are you?" This time minus the "lol": he obviously wasn't laughing out loud any more, and was freaking out at my apparent detective skills.

"Just giving you the heads-up, the sniffer dog's in reception. I'd get that stuff plugged up your balloon knot" (that's your anus, if you were wondering). I feel a bit of an arse looking back, in case he took any of his paranoia out on her. But nothing seems to faze him for long. He messaged me the next day saying, "Hey gorgeous, what was all that about last night, when you coming to see me again?" "Sorry, What?!" I replied.

I'm not even over-exaggerating slightly, he needs help. He texted me a couple of times since when he's been in Manchester and Preston, I've literally just opened my WhatsApp, stared at the phone and rolled my eyes and thought, "Shall I go and meet him orrrrrr shall I moonwalk down the M6?" I know which one's less scary.

CHAPTER FOURTEEN

It was 2015 and Big Brother called again: "Do you fancy going back into the house for a week?" I thought "Yeah, why not, last time was bloody brilliant." They said it would be for a week, but I ended up in there for two.

But God, what a let-down it was this time. I had such an amazing time the first time around that I was excited to be back there, but this house was utterly terrible. Everyone was either super-boring, or had constant ulterior motives, generally through a desperation for fame – here's looking at you Brian Belo Bell-end, and Zippy Nikki Grahame...

The best person in there was Mark O'Neil – we were really close mates in the house, we still are mates today. Me and him and a couple of the other harmless housemates would sit and chat about ordinary mundane stuff, just getting along and having a general light-hearted chit-chat, Mark was such a good character, it was just unfortunate for him that he ended up in the house with a bunch of twats who were there in the hope of making a career off the back of it.

Brian was a right oddball – this was the first time I was meeting him, and he mentioned my tits within five seconds. I felt so uncomfortable around him, and that feeling just kept growing. Within twenty-four hours of being in the house, I went into the diary room and said, "Brian gives off an unnerving presence, do not leave me on my own with him."

When we got up for breakfast the first morning, I was munching a croissant when we came across Brian scrunched up naked in this separate room, with his bum-hole in the air.

"WTF are you doing?"

"Guess what I am?" he said

"Whaaaat, besides a fucking weirdo?"

"I'm a frozen duck – this is what a frozen duck looks like in the freezer."

Right. If I could just eat my croissant in peace now…

Brain massively knows how to play the game, and would storm off, go into bad moods, or go to sleep; looking for everyone to ask him what was the matter. I didn't play along. Blowing smoke up a deluded arse isn't my style.

Brian would bring up conversations that he knew would provoke a reaction from me, and loved turning everything into an argument, but he got more than he bargained for with me.

I humoured his aggression and I fully admit that I'd wind him up AFTER he had come for me. So many of his conversations were really inappropriate, though. He spoke openly about having sex with a really pissed girl out of a hotel window, and was re-enacting the positions in front of us, showing us how he had her bent over in front of him, thrusting away. Hang about, if an older fat guy with jam-jar glasses spoke like this on telly, he would be branded inappropriate and a perv, but no, most of the house found Brian funny.

He also bent one of the female housemates, Harry, over in the middle of the garden and started thrusting and spanking her arse. Why was that ok?

When Ken Morley made comments to Chloe Goodman in a sexual manner he was slated nationwide, torn to shreds by both men and women. He went on Loose Women where they tore him a new arsehole, even though it's ok for that panel of women to touch up naked butlers half their age – tell me that's not double standards! This kind of stuff really winds me up. The whole country turned on him, but I'd seen worse from Brian.

I didn't know until I got out the house, but both Brian and

Zippy Grahame had stood behind the bathroom door one day while me and Mark brushed our teeth, and Brian was saying "He's fingering her, he's definitely fingering her", and she stood there with her old man's testicle for a face, going along with it, knowing full well that wasn't happening; you can clearly hear we were brushing our teeth and talking, but at home you might have believed them. These two were literally a double act, I've never watched two people play a game both while in the house and out of the house, that's all very well and good if you can nail and twist the public's perception to like you when you're not actually a nice person then great, do it, but don't try and frame people and drag people down with you.

While in Big Brother you're not allowed to sleep in the day, but funnily enough, that's all Zippy ever did, unless there was a task or an interesting conversation going on that she knew would be aired. The housemates were all on rations, a chickpea diet, as punishment. I miss that chick-pea diet where my love handles didn't hang over my jeans! I went into the kitchen to try and scavenge some crumbs because I was starving, like everyone else in the house, and there was a separate box in the kitchen full of goodies. "Whose box is this, full of food?" I asked. One of the other housemates said "It's Nikki's" so I opened the box, had a good nosey around it, and what do I find? A big bar of chocolate, among other goodies.

Nikki walked in and obviously questioned why I was rummaging through her stuff. "I thought you were lactose-intolerant, Nikki?"

She said "I am."

"Well, I hate to break it to you, but chocolate contains milk; that's dairy, lactose-intolerant people can't have dairy."

She back-pedalled and said, "I'm only intolerant to some things." (My face is now suffering from severe facial Tourette's). "How the fuck are you only intolerant to some things? You're either lactose-intolerant or you're not, it's one or the other, it's like me saying I'm a vegetarian, but on Tuesday and Thursday I eat cattle."

A lot of housemates, before they go into the house, are divas and Brian Bellends; they have written into their contracts that they're entitled to certain things; personally I think this is absolute bullshit, including Celebrity Big Brother, whether you're a celebrity or not (I am not referring to Nikki or Brian as celebs, as they are not celebrities), unless the likes of Joan Collins goes into that house (she's the only celeb I've stood next to and been starstruck by, she's a goddess) then you shouldn't be entitled to any personal luxuries.

While I loved my Big Brother experience, and am completely grateful for it, Brian and Nikki Grahame live and breathe it. They think they ARE Big Brother, but it's a sodding pantomime and they lose sight of that. Who actually looks up to a reality star? They're just normal people.

The relationship between myself, Bellend and Zippy grew frostier and frostier; that's hardly surprising, we're complete polar opposites; those that watched the show will no doubt remember me saying to Brian one night that he looked like a rapist and a murderer; that all started because we were doing a simple task about questions about who would match who. Brian's was asked "Who would most likely marry for money?" He said me, thinking this would trigger me and upset me but it didn't, I just laughed. By this point I'd figured he had a screw loose, and it's easier to just laugh people like that off or wind them up when they overstep the mark – which he then did.

More questions arose and Brian continued to try and goad me, then he said, "I can't believe you're a mother, you need your throat slitting." I retaliated by saying "Brian, you look like a rapist."

Never bring my son into anything.

Of course when it was aired, you only see my comment. I was presented as the house villain and that's just the way the cookie crumbles; a lot of people said "Are you mad at Big Brother? Have you complained? You need compensation for what everyone is saying about you?" But you put yourself in that position the minute you let them take over your life. And they were my words, nobody made me say that.

That night he went and slept on the floor in the front room. He could have slept in the spare bunker, or the couch, but he slept with a thin blanket next to the stairs.

He knew exactly what he was doing. The next morning everyone was pandering to him like he had slept rough on the town hall steps in the cold, but he was in a warm TV studio and he had decided to sleep on the floor like a stray cat. No one told him to, but remember he knew what would get airtime.

We were all sat in the living area and Brian was still skulking around the garden like a strange bloodhound, walking around and around, when he decided to re-enact Spiderman and scaled the wall; everyone was screaming and shouting, while I casually sat there with Mark drinking my brew, laughing at all these morons going on with themselves. There were probably around twelve fire exits in that house, and the diary room door that leads backstage, but Brian Houdini Belo jumped the wall. People couldn't for some reason see how obvious this was, he was just simply trying to get the sympathy vote.

We all got brought into the living area like a family going to hospital when a grandad dies; to be honest I just wanted to go and have a shower; the housemates sat there holding hands, really close to one another; I was sat there in my towel and I was like "For fuck's sake, I just want a shower, come on," I didn't care about the fact Brian had left. Big Brother announced that Brian had officially left the house (I think we gathered that) and he wouldn't be returning (no shit, Sherlock). I hoped the men in white coats were picking him up on the other side.

Nikki was still in the house; she is a horrible person. Nikki told me a few things off-camera which she had done, which made me think: "You're a piece of shit." She thinks she's a legend, living off Big Brother, wanting people to feel sorry for her; she's four feet tall and like two stone. BY THE WAY, I am not calling the girl for her frame, I am saying her frame is what gets her the sympathy vote; if it was me behaving that way, if she were my height and weight, people would say "Get a grip" and probably give her a slap and say stop feeling sorry for yourself. Your size and how you look can implicate everything.

When Aisleyne Slaggy Claws entered the house she jumped out of a box looking ropey. I wouldn't mind if she was fit but she has a head like a naan bread wearing a fucking Santa hat.

She arrived saying "Basic rations for a basic bitch" and threw a present at me. I said, "Cheers for that, how's Les Dennis?" The Les Dennis comment never got shown on TV but I'm glad I said it, I'm pretty sure a few of you will have seen the picture knocking around of people who are supposedly Aisleyne and Les Dennis in the middle of an orgy in front of her pet chihuahua.

Aisleyne is the most insecure ghetto wannabe I've come across. I spent almost a week with her and I left considering hypnotherapy to see if I could erase the memories of her delusional bad gal attitude. I've never ever in all of my life (thank God) come across a girl who behaves like that.

She was all over every single man in the house day in day out, constantly touching them, but it was the whole accent thing that did it for me; for those of you who don't know, she speaks half Nicki Minaj, half Professor Green, a bizarre combo that drives you mad. Then other times when she tries to get on a level with you she tries to talk like Kate Garraway. She's got more personalities than a character from One Flew Over the Cuckoo's Nest.

While everyone calls me a bully, you have to bear in mind Aisleyne was sent in to "sort me out", for what I'm not too sure; is it fair that someone got sent into the house purposely to upset me?

I might not be the sharpest tool in the box but I can sniff out a rat trying to wind me up the wrong way in order to make me look bad.

The night I was evicted from the house I knew I was going to be booed, that was obvious. I was greeted with a really pissed-off, upset Michelle.

"Don't ever, ever do anything like this again, I can't do it, Helen."

Michelle told me that before the show started, an entertainer got on the stage in front of the audience to gee them all up, he was ordering the audience to act out hanging me with a noose; Michelle had to stand and watch as a few hundred morons did this sick act, I would have laughed usually, but all I could think of was how Michelle felt, stood there watching people act like this towards me. How could Big Brother let their warm-up guy pretend to act out killing me?

Two clients have since told me how they loved me on Big Brother; they made a banner on eviction night and they'd come along for my eviction to cheer me on, but security were confiscating any banners saying, "Helen to win" on them, or "We love Helen."

Now you see why I urge people to stop taking reality TV so seriously; and luckily I let things like that go over my head. But if I was sensitive, or a very anxious person, and I learned people behaved like that towards me, I could have behaved in a very different way. Enacting a noose saying I basically deserved to be dead went a little far, don't you think?

Willis, who is friends with Brian, wouldn't let me get a word in edgeways during my exit interview; I just let her do her thing; it was either that or tell her to go fuck herself. They should have an award for most biased presenter at the TV show awards, Emma would win every year; I just left it and let her crack on with her bullshit; I knew I'd be seeing Rylan next.

He grabbed me and pulled me around the side of the studio, where I smoked a much-needed fag with him; he told me the police were in the studio for my safety, and said: "You've got to apologise Helen, I know you don't want to but people think you said what you said in a racist way."

"What the fuck?"

Bear in mind Brian had left a few days before, which in the house felt like a month ago. I would have said that comment whether he was black, polka-dot, or pasty white with ginger hair. My comments still would have applied; I said what I said because of how he behaved towards me; Rylan said he knew that, but some of the public don't.

We went on stage and I hesitated three times, Rylan glared at me, and I could practically see the message in his eyes: "Apologise, Helen, now."

So I did, and I still stand by the apology; Brian isn't a rapist or a murderer and it wasn't said due to any ethnic reason. How people think it was, I do not know. Every feud I've had in the house in either series I have said equally nasty remarks regardless of a person's skin colour, it's completely out of order that people throw those kind of accusations around.

I don't regret going in for the second time, but since that series I feel there's been a slippery slope. My first time, 2014, was the last good group of people on the show, before it sadly came to an end.

Reality TV is dying a slow death due to snowflake society and the likes of TOWIE. Real people in real situations don't seem to be deemed as entertainment anymore, which is so sad. But RIP to a great house, and I'll always feel blessed I got the chance to go on. The first time it was a ball and a lifelong memory I'll cherish. Even if I changed my mind about some of the housemates afterwards, it was still one of the best summers of my life.

They've just had boring wannabes on the show, I feel it's uninteresting. Get back to people from your 'normal' walk of life, people who work, stop picking people who want a step up to fame.

You can get so wrapped up when you come off the telly, there's money to be made if you want it, there's parties to party at if you want to go, but if you take a good look around you and realise what you have, you don't necessarily want those things. Money is great, let's admit it, but it's not the be all and end all, I was just as happy at winning £100k than I was when I was seventeen/eighteen living in a shit hole, emergency electric about to go, eating spuds and beans. OK magazine wanted a shoot with me when I left Big Brother, but only if I did it with my son, they offered me £7k, is that the price these Z-listers with dodgy reputations shame their kids for?

It's one thing me being known on social media and the odd person recognising me in the street, but to plaster your kid's face, who would have been ten at the time, all over the internet for life? That's fucked up for me. So the shoot didn't go ahead. I'm quite cagey anyway when people talk to me about him, you never know what someone is thinking, plotting, too many strange bodies in the world. I found one scenario quite funny when I'd returned from BB, a lady came over talking to me, said hello to him and said how much we looked alike, we had the same nose and features, he replied "I dunno how, my mum's had a nose job." Lol!

CHAPTER FIFTEEN

My mum lives with me now four or five days of the week and spends weekends with probably the most creditable man I've ever known, really lovely, a one-in-a-million, her boyfriend Ian. He could have walked and I would have understood, but he's stuck by her. I do hope he finds happiness and love with another woman one day, I know he'd always be a friend to my mum in some way, but I've made it clear I'd never have a bad word to say if he moved on. My mum had split up from my dad a good few years ago. Me and Mum started developing a bit of a relationship, and I think that was something to do with him.

Don't get me wrong, we weren't suddenly like best mates or a close mum and daughter, but we were able to be in the same room without things turning into a screaming match within minutes.

She was also really keen to have a closer relationship with my son, and I was happy for that to happen. She would pick him up from school every Thursday and he would stay with her until I was finished at the salon.

One week, though, I was at work when the school rang. Mum had forgotten to pick my son up. I was in the middle of a stressful afternoon as it was, so rang her going insane, but she was really confused. "I don't have him," she kept saying, as though her collecting him on Thursdays was a completely new idea.

I mentioned it to my brother, and he said it wasn't the only odd thing lately, and he was going to get her to the doctor's.

A few days later, Mum rang the salon phone and said she needed to speak to me. I could tell from the tone of her voice that something wasn't right. She hesitated when I asked her what she needed to see me for, and I got a proper sense of dread – I was sure she was going to tell me she had cancer.

I still had a set of eyebrows and four girls that needed

to have a spray tan doing, but I left the shop and went to see her straightaway.

My older brother was already there, and we went into the kitchen and made a brew. Then Mum told me she had Alzheimer's. I didn't actually know that much about what it was, but I did know it meant she was basically dying.

I started acting like I'd popped in for a normal catch-up. I don't know why – it was like my mind decided to block it all out. I don't think I knew how I was supposed to react, or how to handle it.

A few days later, I was back down at her house, acting like everything was hunky-dory, when Mum burst into tears. She started struggling to talk, trying to explain how she felt we'd missed out on so much and she was sorry.

Had she been a good mum? The honest answer is no. Yes, she'd given birth to me, but we had never had a real bond and I had never felt she had my back like a mum should. But from that moment I knew we should never discuss our past. It was over, and not relevant to our lives now. If we were to have any kind of future relationship, it needed to be put to bed.

"There's nothing we can do, we can't change everything that happened," I told her. "There's no point crying, let's make the best of everything from now. You've still got ages left for us to do anything you want to."

Despite saying all that and trying to sound strong, I completely admit the first year or so I couldn't accept my mum was terminally ill. The first time I cried about it was when my mum lost her job. For seventeen years she'd worked at my son's primary school and had built up so many good friends, being there for a long time, the minute her illness was confirmed she lost her job as she was working with children, then in the same week she lost her driving licence; I cried, not because of the Alzheimer's, but because she said: "I have nothing to do now, what am I supposed to do with myself?"

She found out that not only would she soon lose her dignity, but her freedom and independence were disappearing, and that's what upset me. It felt like I was beginning to switch roles with her, and becoming the parent.

Ian, my brother and me were all in agreement that she should be allowed to do anything she wanted if it made her happy. She had lived so much of her life putting up with my controlling dad and the shit he gave her, it was the one thing she deserved.

So Ian took her off on holiday, and I would go shopping with her, and if she wanted to buy something, I was never going to be the one to stop her – even if she already had three of the same tops at home already.

One evening I was making her some dinner and she was chatting to herself in the front room. She pointed at the show she was watching on TV about the Holocaust and said: "I want to go there."

"You want to see where a load of people got gassed?"

"I want to go," she said again.

I could hear her talking to herself about the Holocaust and I thought, why not, if she wants to?

A week later off we went, me, my boy and my mum.

It was the most heart-breaking place I've ever encountered. But there was a positive about going to somewhere that oozes such sadness – my mum became one of us again. Here she was, a woman totally absorbed by one of the most harrowing events of all time, understanding everything that was going on, soaking it up and feeling desperate sadness along with everyone around her.

I worry most of the time that my mum hasn't had enough to drink at home or she might not have eaten her sandwich, but when linking her arms and walking around a gas chamber where mothers and their babies and children were gassed, it made me stop for a second and think "Yeah, my mum is ill but she's happy, and I can look after her, and more importantly we're going to walk out of this gas chamber alive."

It really put things into perspective.

The fact we've actually had the best relationship during her illness is one of the positives to come out of it. Although she hasn't always felt like my mum she has said some of the kindest things she ever said to me, like on my thirtieth birthday she told my friend: "Helen looks SO beautiful." Me and my mum were hardly ever complimentary towards each other when I was growing up, so those few little words meant more to me than anything that night, and that's saying a lot considering I'm the number one fan of getting drunk, dancing and not going home. I treasured a few tiny words and some cheesy dancing with her over any gift I received that day.

Her Alzheimer's has developed pretty rapidly unfortunately, and it has gone from her forgetting the odd person, to needing to be taught how to use a knife and fork to eat a meal, or how to turn the TV on.

I guess I have become like a carer, and some days I handle it fine, others not so much. It can be the little situations that I struggle with.

Recently, Ian and Mum were going to a party and I went round to help her get ready. It was a black-tie do with sixties and seventies music, and I knew she would love it. It's the kind of place where she really comes back out of her shell, and she can dance for hours.

I helped her into the shower and went to help her shave her legs as she was going to wear a dress, and she kept pushing my hand away: "No!"

So I handed her the razor, but she stood with it, doing nothing.

"Stand up and let me shave your legs. You need to do this!"

She started going bananas and shouting at me, and I stood there, thinking what am I doing? I can't be arsed. I've worked all day, and now I'm trying to make you look nice, so you can feel like your old self for one evening. I just didn't know what to do, as she was my mum, she deserved respect, but at the same time the only way to get her to behave was to talk to her like a toddler. She was responding like a child, so even though it was difficult, that's what I did.

Then we got into her room and she didn't want to wear this gorgeous dress, she wanted to wear a woolly jumper. It was twenty-two degrees outside, and I knew the minute she got to the do and was wearing something completely different to everyone else, she'd feel alienated.

"Fine, don't go to the party!" I told her, and she sulked.

Maybe some people would say I should have let her do what she wanted, but I know the real her would have wanted to look right, and look her best. It is like being cruel to be kind.

Finally, she wore the dress, put some red lippy on, and went off happy as could be with Ian, who told me they had the best night ever.

But I sat home and cried, because I hated the way I had spoken to her, and felt guilty.

It is so hard to talk about, and I know my friends have tried to be supportive, but unless you've lived through it, you never fully understand.

I did feel for my mum, as she wanted to help me and do things for me, I had friends who had babies in their teens and their mums were able to do so much. I craved that relationship with my mum when my son was born, I always wanted her to ask if she could have my son, make a fuss of him, like nannas do, but it was always me asking if she could have him, which then turned into more trouble than it was worth. She would get stick for helping me out, both from my dad and her sisters. Nobody ever wanted me and my mum to be close, only now, now Mary's died and we're left with a shell, everyone's happy for me to have a relationship with her.

The Alzheimer's has taken over, I don't remember when I spoke to Mary herself, which isn't really a bad thing as we weren't a loving mum and daughter anyway. I'm like a closed book at the moment when it comes to emotions, because I find it quite hard to stomach. Truth is, my mum made a comment years back about how she'd rather go into a home than have me care for her. We were very bitchy towards one another, I remember thinking and feeling pretty shit at that comment, she didn't know me as a daughter or as a person to say that, because she'd only ever seen me angry or upset, running away, she saw me as a problem, she had no idea how much I'd give to help her if she ever needed it.

When my mum was diagnosed, my name wasn't on anything regarding the legalities for her, which at the time I wasn't fussed about, but only recently when things have been tough, I've blocked out the fact she's signed papers basically saying she doesn't trust me with her life, only my brothers, now as much as I'm thick-skinned at the best of times, that is a bit of a kick in the teeth when the whole family have deserted her.

Even now when my mum is poorly, she's still at the mercy of men who think only about themselves. I have no legal say in where she goes and my brother wants her in a home. I'm trying to keep her with me for as long as I can, but a man, a selfish, nasty arsehole who she should be able to trust with her life and well-being, her son, is ready to ship her off into care. He can't cope with the state she is in, so it's easier to toss her to one side and let others deal with her.

The only man she could ever trusted, her current boyfriend, has had no say or support from the rest of the family. To me he's a hero who's been ignored and disregarded, I hope he finds happiness once my mum's sons have decided her fate!

I don't want recognition for looking after her, what I want is impossible, not obtainable, I wanted her to know the real me and how much I'd have looked after her when she was sane, but there's no use wishing for the impossible, I have and do still intend to make the most of what time we have left together. I have days where I feel severely trapped because I'm envisioning a different life, but I'm happy most of the time. My son, friends, and also travelling a lot with work, balances out the shitty days.

For someone with a weak mentality like Mum I fully appreciate having a daughter who is the polar opposite must have been challenging, so we called a truce. She was a shit mum, I perhaps wasn't an easy daughter, let's move on. I'll never fully understand why the fuck both sets of parents put myself and my brothers at risk. You don't have to be a parent to know that's just callous.

There will be flashes of the old her, when we've sat silently in a restaurant over food, and then she suddenly starts chatting about someone we both know, or a memory from the past. Sometimes she'll show a moment of real empathy or do something daft or funny that's like a happier version of her old self. If there's one positive to this grim fucking condition, it's that wiping her memory seems to have wiped all the shit she went through with my dad. So a lot of the memories that maybe weighed her down, have actually gone.

I've always been a massive supporter of animal charities and since my mum got diagnosed with Alzheimer's it's made me realise how ignorant I've been towards charities in the past; now, although I don't have umpteen direct debits coming out every month helping umpteen charities, I do take more notice of those that are less fortunate, whether it be health, life in general, the homeless, etc. I embarrassingly used to have a really shit attitude towards people who were homeless. I used to think they were all alcoholics and it was their own fault – that stigma is something I grew up around, but I've learned over the years that not everything is what it seems.

I got a homeless man and a dog some food not long ago; it was pissing down of rain, the homeless man had taken off his jacket and put it over his dog; it was his own coat; how does a man who has absolutely nothing have that much of a heart? I've grown a lot more sensitive as I've got older towards people needing things. This isn't some lame shot at me trying to come across as the next Mother Teresa, I'm not the type of person that would do lots of charity and voluntary work, but I do feel as I'm getting older I have more responsibility to try and change things instead of ignoring them.

So I decided to raise some money for the Alzheimer's Society, and I agreed to do something crazy: I signed up to climb

Kilimanjaro at the end of 2016, I mean how hard could it be?

There was a group of us doing it together, and well, while the rest of them trained ... I didn't. Because getting fit for it was something I'd been told to do, my stubborn streak meant I didn't. Talk about cutting my nose off to spite my face! While they were all off exercising, I spent the run-up to Christmas drinking, eating, smoking, and sat on my arse. It's one of the most stupid things I've ever done.

Then on Boxing Day, thirty-three of us set off on what should have been the epic trip of a lifetime...

It was quite amusing at the start; both myself and my Kilimanjaro buddy Yva were having a laugh, everyone was taking it in their stride, walking up what could be called a hill that took us to the gate of Kilimanjaro, when we both looked at each other and I just gasped and said: "I'm not being funny, but I'm fucked already." We'd only been walking for twelve sodding minutes. We both just started laughing, we straightaway had a bond – we were certainly the divas.

Sadly for all of us, and I'm sure I can speak on everyone's behalf, the weather ruined our experience; I can't say I enjoyed it, that would be a big fat lie; our tents and sleeping bags were drenched, we slept for only three to six hours a night, from say ten p.m. to four a.m., and then it's climbing non-stop from the moment you wake up; I never quite realised how strong-willed I am as a person until I faced this challenge and refused to give up.

The idea was, we were going to get to the summit on New Year's Eve. What a way to end the year! I envisioned us all sat at the top of this amazing mountain that God created, around a camp fire, singing 'Kumbaya', eating marshmallows. Needless to say, it was fuck-all like that.

We woke up at one a.m., after fourteen hours of climbing in the snow the day before, and just two hours' sleep. We had a bowl of dry cold pasta to prepare us for the summit, then eleven of us set off – most of the camp had dropped like hot cakes over the past five days, through being severely ill and needing to be sent back down.

By now, I was suffering really badly from altitude sickness. My stomach was in total agony, and I was being sick everywhere. I felt really spaced out, and someone gave me tablets to help – but the side effect was worse: diarrhoea. After not being able to go to the toilet for the first three days, I was farting and shitting in front of everyone while basically wailing – I no longer cared.

There was this Scouse woman who was my absolute rock and kept me going: "Come on girl!" But then I collapsed. Kilimanjaro is 5,895 metres above sea level and I was just 300 bloody metres from the summit, when my body gave up on me.

Some really nice Tanzanian guys wrapped me up like a cocoon and ran down 500 metres with me so I could get a rush of oxygen. I felt I had a rush of life and asked to carry on, but the doctor said I wasn't allowed to because I'd collapsed. I was angry, and determined, but she was adamant.

The only plus side was going down meant feeling better. I'd happily give birth to ten ten-pound babies than put myself through the altitude sickness again.

Other than that though, I hated the descent. I kept veering off on my own route, which probably took me longer, but I was just so angry. I kept joking with a friend about faking injury to get airlifted off – and then she really did fall and mess up her knee and elbow. Thank God an ambulance came and picked us up!

As if things couldn't get worse, by the time I got to the bottom I had started my period and didn't have any tampons, so I'd doubled up on underwear. I waddled over the finish line stinking and crying my eyes out, sure I was never going to be stupid enough to do anything like this again in my life…

Until you've done something like this you'd never know how it feels to get so close, but then not quite make it; members of the team were saying if you get to 5,000 feet you can say you've done it; it's funny now, but it took me a while to see the funny side right then. I did climb that mountain!

The best part was I thought my mum would have no idea where I'd been for two weeks, but when I got back she saw me pull up on her drive and came out with the biggest smile on her face, saying, "Oh, you're back, you've been up that mountain."

I cried that she knew where I'd been, and I could show her the photos and videos.

"You didn't have to do that," she said.

Wow, she even remembered why I'd done it! Was she faking this illness to make me climb a mountain? I laughed. "Bloody selective memory, you. But it's ok. I wanted to do it."

And somehow it seems I've signed up to walk the Great Wall of China for October 2019, so watch this space, ha ha!!!

CHAPTER SIXTEEN

It's not a nice thing to admit this but I did really start to get fucked off with men, I grew to be quite cold, kinda like well this is it now, everyone knows what I've done thanks to a man not saving my ass when I was prepared to save his (Wayne). I began not giving a shit about what people thought, I still don't but not to the degree where it's festering inside and I'm bitter, I became bitter towards men again. Max Clifford was EXCELLENT at making me believe I was some form of victim, that men had taken advantage, the irony of this man ever slating another man's wrongdoing towards a woman is 'almost' laughable.

After Ash I took a complete backseat from men for a while, apart from male friends I didn't take anyone on board whatsoever and it's been the best thing I could have done (I think), although sometimes I'm a bit too standoffish and even when I might be attracted to a guy, which is very rarely, I don't show it at all, so then they friend-zone me and shag my mate. I SHOULD be out dating, experimenting, testing the water, but the truth is I've found it a lot easier to close myself off. I've dipped my toe into the water a few times, but it never seems to work, and just makes me pull back into myself, like "See? I told you it wouldn't work!"

There was one guy I went on a few dates with, that just felt like good, long-overdue fun; he was really nice and dead funny, but then we both went away on separate holidays, and I had a gut feeling he had taken another bird away, so I didn't bother messaging him; then my phone rang, a friend was randomly in the same place on holiday as him, and I just knew what she was going to say – she had just seen the guy with his missus, who it turned out she also knew. Slightly awkward for him... I couldn't help but laugh – what else can you do?

I thought that would be the last I heard from the cheeky sod, then I got a text: "How's your holiday, babe?" I simply replied: "Amazing, thanks, I heard yours is good too."

Then I met a guy in Ibiza. I literally thought BINGO: he was tall, dark, handsome, well into Ibiza, music and travel, and he was Irish. I thought the Irish are usually really good to get along with and I told him that I work in Dublin sometimes so we arranged to meet up; however, it was literally like another episode of Question Time. This guy was like an interrogator, asking me every single question imaginable, asking me about my past and what I wanted for my future; I envisioned going out, getting pissed with a fit Irish guy, having a laugh and spending a boozy weekend together. I think I would have had more fun with Roy Cropper.

Goes to show you can't have it all; and he was waaaaay too into himself; I'm absolutely NOT into men who look in a mirror more times than me.

The cheeky swine also sent me a text when I came home to say his ex-bird had sent him a newspaper clipping of me; first of all, why on earth did she know about me, why had he told her, and secondly, who is anyone to send me a newspaper clipping due to something that happened almost a decade ago? I found it really bizarre. Maybe I should have offered my services. I messaged him and said if you've got any questions and if you want to know what's true or not, I've got a book coming out, go buy yourself a copy...

It isn't the only time I've had that reaction either. Once a date finds out who I am, it's like it turns into a therapy session. They'll tell me: "I want you to know I'm ok about your past."

You what? I didn't ask if you were! Have I quizzed you on your past and sat in judgement on it? No! Because you had a life before me and it's none of my business. But unfortunately, because my past is out there, it's like everyone thinks they're entitled to an opinion on it. It's horrible, because it means no relationship ever starts on even ground.

I probably do carry the hurt about it deeper than I like to admit, and it's one of the main things that stops me getting into a new relationship. I'm petrified a bloke would throw my past in my face one day, and that would be the end of it. It might be six weeks into a relationship, or six years down the line, but if it came out in a row, and it was clear they had held that thought all that time, I'd never be able to forgive them, or myself for putting myself in that position.

But while I might not want to be in a relationship at the minute, that doesn't mean I don't want sex. I have a high sex drive, and sex is important to me, but because of the way I feel about men at the minute, I get very little of it!

So, one day just for fun I looked into getting a gigolo... I thought it could be the answer. Hire one every few months to keep me ticking over and he won't ask questions, he's not gonna pry, it's a business deal.

I contacted a guy who had been employed by several models and actresses, so that kind of convinced me he'd be the right one for the job. WRONG: when I asked him how much he rented his penis out for, he replied with his rate, and added: "I understand if you don't want the whole night because you've got a kid."

To me this made it obvious he was an amateur in the industry; you don't tell your clients how much you rent your nether region out for, then mention their child in the same sentence. I gave him a friendly tip about that for the future.

Unbelievably he replied: "It's okay, I understand, hun." Ugh, I hate the word "hun", especially from a guy. That word alone would merit the booking being cancelled.

Within the space of a few minutes I'd gone from texting a gigolo, to being informed how much his dick cost while being reminded I have a child in the same sentence, to being called "hun".

I was beginning to feel like Jim in American Pie and was seriously doubting this idea. I looked at his picture again – muscles and a torso five times flatter than mine.

I consume thirty-six Jaffa cakes two to three times a week, I drink plenty of white wine, I don't take carbs into consideration whatsoever, and I smoke menthols when I want to be thin. Fuck it, I decided, I couldn't lie in bed with a guy with a body like a Ken doll. I would end up feeling body-shamed and end up doing squat thrusts instead of having sex. Give me a dad bod any day. I needed a different solution…

Instead I went to see a therapist about curbing my needs, as well as learning how to relax and not be so frosty around guys; it's good to listen to advice from someone totally out of your circle, they're completely neutral; it's hard talking to friends who are all married or have long-term boyfriends and have never lived alone; they don't quite grasp what it's like not to have that interaction.

I think the key for me is being one hundred per cent comfortable in my own company, which I can say I am these days. Although I manage to fuck up the basic things in life like booking a flight or catching a train on time, I'm comfortably self-sufficient. Sometimes a little too much, because the thought of a man sharing any form of responsibility with me freaks me out. Those recent dates had both taken me out for something to eat and it made my toes curl when they paid for the meals. It's daft, as I do believe a man should pay for the meal on a date, but when I'm sat there I feel really different.

The other thing that I'm paranoid about with dates is, I know I'm a bit of a weirdo in lots of ways, and I might freak men out! So, like some people mightn't like the colour of the walls in a restaurant, but they will just ignore it. I can't, I have to leave. I'm not a diva, it literally drives me mad and I need out, but what is the guy with me going to think about that?

I have no idea what the future holds for me with men really. My son is at a crucial age where I don't want to introduce him to just anyone, and we're happy as we are anyway.

I don't think, Oh God, I need to get married, but I'd like to, if I met the right person. I'd also think about having more kids with that person. I can't think of anything more attractive in a man than watching them protect, help, and love their own child. I'd like a daughter and to be the person for her that I never had. I'd show her that she is my everything, and no matter what, she will always have someone who has her back.

I would also love to foster. I knew from a young age after being in the fostering world myself, that once I was in the position to give back, I'd be making sure it was first on my agenda. But I've begun looking into it lately, and it's not exactly turned out as I hoped. While being on TV was great, it has turned out to be a massive hindrance, blocking people from seeing what I'm actually like as a person in private – a mother, a friend, and someone who wants to help. It seems that the agencies aren't able to see past what they've seen onscreen and read in the papers, and so far, I've been knocked back by four of them.

I had one lady come to see me, who spent the best part of three or four hours in my company and told me how she'd be giving positive feedback to the panel in charge. It was only when I told her about Big Brother and the bollocks with the newspapers years ago, that everything went wrong. I got the cold shoulder and was ignored.

I continued to apply with other agencies, one of which asked me to go ahead with the application after me explaining about my colourful past, but then three meetings in, I heard nothing, zilch. Another agency spoke to me as though I was a convicted paedo when giving me the verdict on my application, and the fourth agency explained how a child would be at risk because people know who I am. I thought this was a piss-poor excuse – there's TV programs with foster carers on them, Lydia Bright's mum from TOWIE talks openly about her role as a foster mum, etc., so they can't tell me I don't have the love, commitment and stability to offer a child because I took part in a game show.

It feels like the childcare system is set up to keep a child in an environment that's not suitable, that is mentally or physically damaging, over giving a caring person a chance to make a difference.

Plenty of people make mistakes, plenty of people have another side to them, we all do. Yes, I know I swear, I'm vocal, and I may come across as aggressive at times, but this is usually when you've got some berk adult getting on your last nerve. That is completely different from a child in need who feels rejected, let down, and has never felt safe. To be told I can't contribute to making a difference to their life because of something I did a decade ago, and because I participated in a reality TV programme, baffles me.

I'd like to think I've grown myself a skin as thick as a rhino's when it comes to being misunderstood or knocked back for things, but it's really felt like a kick in the teeth.

My dream would be to change just one child's life and I am determined I will foster one day, but for now, it's something that is out of my hands.

It has been weird writing this book. I don't think many people can say they've lived through a life quite like mine, or experienced anything like a fraction of what I have in my thirty-two years on this earth!

When I'm writing about the early bits, not wanting to sound like a cliché, but it's like I'm talking about a different person.

I grew up in a life where domestic violence was the norm, where verbal or physical abuse was accepted, and where toxic energy was all around. If someone hit me or sexually abused me now I'd be confused and question why. But for most of my life I was numb, and thought that was just what happened. After all it was a man's world, so there were no rules to stop those things happening to me.

I think when I was younger, I just wanted peace. I'm much closer to having that now, and it is still what I work towards. I used to be such a stresshead – like I put not just the one 's' in stress, but all three of them – but I've mellowed and grown resilient.

When you've lived a toxic episode in life, or in my case a full series, there's no better feeling than looking back and thinking: who the fuck was that? Although I've not changed in a lot of ways, the bad things have turned into good, every single bit of shittiness has somehow turned out to have added value to my life.

In terms of other future plans, I want to travel more, with my son, with friends, and by myself. I love my own company and I've finally found that venturing out and doing things by yourself makes you take a step back from searching for things that will come naturally.

And honestly – although I don't know how it will ever happen – I'd like to live a lot more of an anonymous life. That might sound weird, after all the press I've done over the years, and the fact that I'm writing this.

But I never wanted to be in the public eye. It was just when my hand was forced, I thought the only choice I had was to try and take some control over it. To have my say.

In an ideal world, no one would know about me.

People ask why I'm dragging it up now – for me this isn't dragging it up, it's my everyday life. Not a day goes past without someone asking about it, mentioning it on Twitter, passing me in the street and thinking it's their place to comment...

People who follow me on Twitter will most likely often see the jibes about Catholicism, religion, priests etc. I get that I offend innocent people who believe in these religions, I mean no malice towards them, honestly. Truth is, a priest severely abused a close relative of mine, to the point this had a knock-on effect on our lives. Back in the day it was all hush-hush when priests were heard to be doing things, this person told nobody for a long time, but it massively fucked them up and had a massive impact on my life as well as on others in the family.

So all this being said, I was still urged by the family to be an altar server, and I've never, ever been able to fathom why my mum put me at risk like this: why would you drop your daughter off with a priest an hour before Mass is to start, knowing they're in that church alone with a priest? This kinda shit annoys me and still does, my mum's very sick yes, but I'd be lying if I didn't say there was some form of resentment there.

My son was getting in trouble in his second year of school. He came home to tell me that once a week he was to go and talk to a priest, this went down like a fart in church with me, hell would freeze over before I okayed a non-professional man of God to take my son to one side. I wouldn't allow Simon the window cleaner to start counselling my kid, a priest with no qualification wouldn't be doing this either, it's barmy. I'm not for one second saying all priests are bad eggs, but as a mother, why take the risk? I wouldn't.

I took my son out for his birthday to an Italian restaurant and a group of lads on another table started chanting: "Rooney! Rooney! Rooney!"

Trying to intimidate me years on from what happened, and in front of my son, is wrong, which they realised afterwards, when they tried to send over a bottle of champagne in apology. But I face stuff like that every day. Trolls, who threaten to find my son and tell him exactly what they think of his mother. What kind of people are these?

I don't know what some people want from me. It's like their goal in life is to see me crumble, a girl who they've never met. But I don't crumble, and never will, and that seems to make them madder.

You only have to look at the coverage of me to see just how much of a man's world it is. Even promoting this book, I was taken to task by Jeremy Kyle on Good Morning Britain. He didn't have any interest in what I actually had to say, but just talked over me, clearly taking the side of his pal Wayne. Invite the woman on, but don't let her have a voice. Luckily, so many people saw that, and I came off air to at least four thousand messages of support on Instagram.

I'd love all of this to be in my past, but no one else will let it stay there. Maybe with this book I'll get some kind of closure.

I didn't start all this, but I am attempting to finish it.

I'm a woman who has made mistakes, mistakes that I'm fully responsible for, but name me one person who hasn't ballsed up a few times, the difference being my mistakes won't ever be forgotten. That's why I've had to say my piece – where as in most cases when people mess up they can move on, erase it, block it out, it's a way of life I've become accustomed to.

Mind you, there's been one massive silver lining; I've grown skin as thick as a rhino's, I don't take any prisoners and I cherish my son and my friends dearly. Bad things happen but they can bring out the best in you, that's how I see it, I'm just working on bringing down my barriers a little more before I turn into a 50-year-old spinster collecting cats and thimbles. Of course, there's something missing, but I won't rush or force things. For now my son, my mum and my friends are more than a lot of people have, so I'm grateful for that.

Some names have been changed to protect the privacy of individuals.